Bobby Short

THE LIFE AND TIMES OF A Saloon Singer

THE LIFE AND

A Panache Press Book

CLARKSON POTTER/PUBLISHERS

NEW YORK

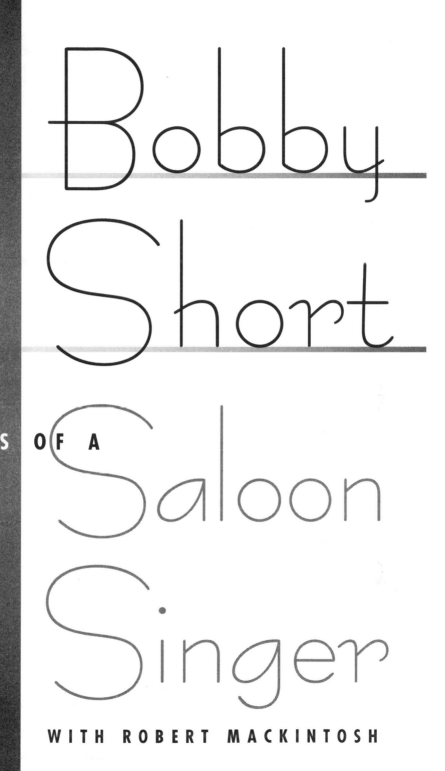

Bobby Short

TIMES OF A

Saloon Singer

WITH ROBERT MACKINTOSH

Owing to limitations of space, permission acknowledgments can be found on page 266, which constitutes an extension of this copyright page.

Published by Clarkson Potter/Publishers, 201 East 50th Street, New York, New York 10022. Member of the Crown Publishing Group.

Random House, Inc. New York, Toronto, London, Sydney, Auckland

CLARKSON N. POTTER, POTTER, and colophon are trademarks of Clarkson N. Potter, Inc.

Manufactured in the United States of America

Design by Jane Treuhaft

Library of Congress Cataloging-in-Publication Data
Short, Bobby.
    Bobby Short, the life and times of a saloon singer / by Bobby Short
with Robert Mackintosh.
       p.   cm.
      1. Short, Bobby. 2. Singers—United States—Biography.
I. Mackintosh, Robert G. II. Title.
ML420.S539A3   1995
782.42164'092—dc20
[B]   95-6978
                          CIP

ISBN 0-517-59564-8

10 9 8 7 6 5 4 3 2 1

First Edition

Acknowledgments

My warmest thanks to Jean Bach, William Claxton, Edward Collins, Thomas Quinn Curtis, Marjorie Downey, Maur Dubin, Rodolphe d'Erlanger, Carl Galm, Sonja Gilbert, Stephane Grappelli, Marguerite Graves, Peter Howard, James H. Hulse, Robert Kimball, Marguerite Littman, David Long, H. Scollard Maas, Julius Monk, Tom Parr, Isabelle Powell, James de Priest, Jean Sablon, Daisy Taylor, Mary Whelan Warburg, Elisabeth Welch, and Preston Young for their eager cooperation in helping to fill some of the blank spots in my memory.

I am also deeply indebted to Burl Stiff who researched for me in Southern California and to Chris Milner who at the beginning of this project mined the libraries of Paris, France, for information about Paris in the twenties and thirties.

To my assistant, Christina Wyeth, infinite gratitude for the work involved in completing this endeavor and many thanks also to the late Fred Graves for the hours he spent typing my early manuscripts.

My thanks to Editor-at-Large Betty A. Prashker and to Jane Treuhaft, Amy Boorstein, Joy Sikorski, and Cressida Connolly at Crown for the care, attention, and expertise they have given this book. I could not be more grateful.

Finally, I shall be indebted forever to my friend and editor, Geraldine Stutz, without whose insistence and guidance this book would never have seen the light of day.

For Nelliegray Brown

Not bad, Mr. Short." I give one last tug to the loop of my tie for a less-than-perfect knot. Slightly off kilter; if I wanted a tie that was absolutely symmetrical, I might as well wear a clip-on. Now a pull at the handkerchief tucked in my breast pocket. "No, not bad at all." I am talking to myself in front of the mirror before I go downstairs for the second show. Saturday night, and my last one of the spring season here at the Hotel Carlyle.

What I am getting in the mirror may not be accurate, but oh boy, is it reassuring. A diffused image. Well, the tie is right, the suit is pressed, the shirt is pristine—and thanks to my tyrant trainer, Mike Iozzino, I'm in pretty good shape.

Now to ride three floors down to the lobby in the quiet elevator. There is nothing that is not attractive at the Carlyle. The gentle light, the gray-blue panels . . . and I have the elevator all to myself. From nowhere the thought pops into my head—Mr. Short, you have been riding in front elevators for a long time now.

Across the lobby, the gleaming black-and-white marble floors give a reflection as I walk. The gun-metal

3

lusters of the crystal chandeliers shimmer below my feet.

I pass the mirrors with their exotic ormolu frames. Through the red lounge, all Turkish and chinoise. Crimson and scarlet, claret and burgundy. Fabric-covered walls, painted screens. Pattern on pattern. Now up the few steps—on red carpet—and out to the vestibule facing Madison Avenue. To the Cafe Carlyle. A young fellow and his girl come rushing through the revolving door. "Bobby, you haven't gone on yet?" Wide smiles of relief. "We thought we might be late."

No, I was not going on for another few minutes. What a satisfactory moment for a performer. Fans—afraid they might lose their table. And a cool, late spring breeze from the street came through the door with them.

Ambrose stands at his maître d' station near the entrance. He is the man who answers the phone and takes down the reservations, he seats the customers, pours the wine, and sometimes mixes the salad dressing. Soothing ruffled nerves is often his job, too. Now with a big pleased-with-himself grin he says, "We are sold out."

Sold out. For anyone in my business, the two most beautiful words in the world.

In a minute there will be Robb Scott's drumroll, Beverly Peer's thump on the bass, signaling my entrance. The Marcel Vertes satyrs and nymphs, all pink and pale, are floating and prancing along the walls as usual. And at the bar there is a customer at each of the dozen bar stools; it looks like another twelve are standing. Behind the bar Sal and Domingo are smiling, too. I am ready to walk to the piano.

What they do in movies is called a lap dissolve. You are in a scene one second and then in a flash you are some place else. Maybe life is a series of film clips, short scenes popping in and out of view. Pictures of Then and Now.

The Now is that I am off for the summer. In the morning I pack up the last of my clothes, I zip up the luggage and leave for France. For Provence. I will be in my house in Mougins the day after tomorrow.

There goes Beverly's bass; Robb's hands are poised in midair, ready to hit the drums. Everyone is aware that tonight marks twenty-five years here in this marvelous, sometimes madhouse, but always welcoming room. I walk toward the piano—and the first time I stepped up on this little stage is suddenly as clear to me as if it were only yesterday. On comes the always encouraging sound of applause.

And there it is, another flash. Another yesterday— the Then, when I shut the clasp on the valise my mother had packed before I took off for those first bookings out of Danville, Illinois, in the depths of the Depression.

Danville
1936

A plastic suitcase, black-and-white herringbone pattern with a black stripe across the center—to look like a strap with a buckle. I can see it. Mother's suitcase looked quite spiffy. Like her clothes, like our house.

I never knew how she did it without money, but that house on North Robinson Street in Danville was always shining. The parlor with oak furniture and Leatherette upholstery. The ugliest furniture in the world, but somehow it all had style. A davenport with oak feet and arms, matching chairs, a bookcase. And at the end of the room an ebony-finished upright piano. As soon as I could walk across the parlor floor I found the Walworth; at age four I stood there playing "Who Stole My Heart Away," the Jerome Kern song. In the dining room there was an oak table with a white runner on it. Usually new. When something in a store caught Mother's fancy, she somehow managed to scrape together the money to buy it. Like white cotton lace runners for the table, like curtains on all the windows—and records for the oak Victrola.

Like her black-and-white suitcase. And her clothes. She always wore a hat and gloves, little gold earrings, her hair marcelled with a knot at the back of her neck. She never cut it. No new-style bob for her. "You can cut your hair the day I shave off my mustache," my father had said. And he wore the mustache all his life.

His life began in Rockport, Kentucky, and then the town of Frankfurt, where he went to high school. My mother loved to announce that she had married an educated man. I can see him sitting across from me at the dining room table. My book was open in front of me, and he was reading aloud, though the words were upside down. That was magic for me—Mother was right to brag about him.

Preceding page: A twelve-year-old in tails—my first professional studio portrait.

9

Mama and Papa—
Myrtle and
Randell Short.

After he finished school he came to Danville to work in the mine. That was long before I was born, but I knew he had been a mailman, served as a notary public and justice of the peace. He even owned an ice-cream parlor for a time. Some of the sherbet dishes, spoons, and ice-cream scoops were still in the kitchen drawer; my favorite seat was a curving metal chair, and one of the spoons was my special property. I never knew why he abandoned the ice-cream parlor, but he went back to mining, and when there was no work available in Danville, he went down to Lynch, Kentucky. I guess mining was the only job he ever liked. It was the job that killed him.

Papa came up to Danville whenever he could, which wasn't too often, never more than twice a year. But he kept in touch with birthday presents, sometimes a set of china or clothes for Mother and the tins of sorghum that she loved and could not find in

Danville. Twice a month he mailed a check, sometimes for twenty-five dollars, sometimes only eight or nine, depending on the work at the mine. Mama was hired as a domestic, and my sister Naomi took over the chores of housekeeping.

Naomi was the eldest in a line of ten. Six of us lived. Ruth died at fifteen, run over by a car on Main Street. Twin boys had died at birth, and then came Mildred, followed by Charles William and Roberta, who died when she was three or four days old. Reginald was next; Mama said his name came to her in a dream. Then I was born—and last of all was Barbara Louise.

Those few times a year when my father came home there was a special excitement in the house and a party or two for his cronies with the home brew that he had made on his last trip brought out. It was the only time I heard words like "damn" and "hell"; such words were forbidden when he was away. He called me his million-dollar baby with the million-dollar smile, and he never forgot my birthday, but I thought of him as a visitor. So did little Barbara.

The Depression had hit hard; no job was too menial if it brought in much needed money. Mildred was the local reporter for the *Chicago Defender*, one of the oldest Negro newspapers in the country, and I'd pick up a few pennies making deliveries. Reg got odd jobs in town and sold magazines; Bill shined shoes, cut grass, and learned how to press clothes.

But there were church suppers and school assemblies, and I was singing, learning every song that excited me. Somehow Mama managed to find the twenty-five cents necessary for Mrs. Helene Smith's piano lessons. Mrs. Smith was patient teaching me the exercises, drilling me in the basic scales and how to read music. I went through the lessons and played back whatever she had played. Imitation came easy to me, and soon Mrs. Smith was teaching me how to walk on a stage, how to bow and address an audience for my first appearance at the Second Baptist Church recital.

My memory of that momentous occasion is crystal clear. I

began with "I will now play the 'Firefly Waltz,'" moved to the piano, and placed the sheet music on the rack. I never looked at it, and I played the piece from first note to last without taking my eyes off the audience.

Not long after, I was playing in the local saloons. In those days, before I was in my teens, I was led in and out of the Danville bars, from roadhouse to roadhouse, wherever there was a private party. The taverns in those Depression years were not always full, not even on weekends. Sometimes at one of the places on the edge of town I would fall asleep at the piano during a lull, with my head on my arms, until the glare of headlights flashed through the windows. They'd wake me, and by the time the customers got to the door I'd be up and singing "Nobody's Sweetheart," or "Nagasaki," or "Tiger Rag."

Sleepy or not—I was bringing home a couple of dollars. A few of the local citizens steered me around town, taking their share of what I earned—and I took what I was given with no questions asked, happy to make my contribution at home.

That summer of 1936 the American Legion had come to town for their convention, and a week-long jamboree it was: parades with bands playing and flags waving, a patriotic procession turning into a drunken free-for-all. Night after night that week I was out in the fray, with a man named Porter Hudson leading me from one bar to another, to impromptu spots called dugouts—a nod to the trenches of World War I—and in the Hotel Wolford ballroom he passed the hat after I finished a performance. Then in the bright and rowdy early morning I was sitting in an old steam-driven calliope out in the street—everyone in town was cleaning up from the Legionnaires' spending spree, and Porter saw to it I was earning our share.

The next morning a young fellow appeared at our front door, a singer named Leonard Rosen who was booked at the convention and had heard me the night before. A friend named Julius Levin

With my sister Barbara and Pal, the family pet of no particular pedigree, in front of our house on Robinson Street.

was with him—an agent, he was called Bookie and he was from Joliet. They wanted to talk to my mother about taking me to work in Chicago.

Mother was not at home, but I knew where to find her and we drove to the house where she was doing her half day. I listened to Bookie's sales pitch—how talented I was, what a great future I had, and Mrs. Short, think of the money your boy could be sending home. This was going to need some thought, she said, and would they come over for dinner?

They plied me with ice cream and malts and candy that afternoon. They painted a splendid picture of work at the finest nightclubs and in radio, the movies, and the best vaudeville houses.

Hours later at home I could tell Mother was asking herself questions; I knew her wide eyes meant she was waiting for a decision from me—at eleven I was expected to be sure of myself.

"Do you want to go?" she asked me.

Did I! Well, of course I could hardly wait.

So she was packing my shirts and underwear and the necessities she thought of at the last moment—giving me a big kiss, a bit of money, and a warning about how to behave.

I've got my eyes on you, so best beware where you roam . . ." It seems just a beat ago that I began my opening number. "Don't stray too far from home . . ." And here I am finishing the last phrase: "Just be wise, keep your eyes on me!"

Eyes were on me as soon as Bookie Levin and Len Rosen drove me to Joliet, where they lived. Bookie had business to tend to, and he left me with Len in the lobby of the Woodruff Hotel. Two gray-haired ladies who were admiring me could not help asking questions, and my answers were quick and not without bragging.

"I'm going to work here in Joliet, ma'am. I play the piano and sing."

"Why, how sweet. And could you play a piece for us?"

"Yes, I'd be delighted to." And off I went to the cocktail bar with two elderly ladies. God knows what they expected—what they got was "Love is like a cigarette . . . I never felt the thrill of love until I touched your lips."

At first I stayed with Len Rosen's mother, but the apartment was crowded, so I was moved over to Bookie's parents' house. The two families could not have been kinder while Bookie worked hard to promote his new find—Bobby Short.

It sounded like a B movie hearing him talk to Len after one of my first jobs. "So how's the kid? How'd the kid do out there?"

Right off a white tail suit was made for me, and they sorted out my material in preparation for the big "new act."

"Sell it, sell it!" In vaudeville houses—at night in cocktail lounges, Len Rosen was there, directing my bows, telling me when to give the crowd an encore. "Smile, smile!" He saw that I was clothed and fed, that I had haircuts and clean laundry.

Soon he was sending money home for me. We had lots of club dates—meaning one-night stands. In hotels, for conventions, and at lodge get-togethers. I worked in Chicago, and then we hit the road. St. Louis, Milwaukee, Kansas City. Cleveland and Kenosha, Wisconsin. I had reviews in *Variety*—good ones that Len sent home to Mother.

They took me to New York, where the child labor laws required me to have a tutor—at twenty dollars a week. Bookie gave her fifteen. I was booked into the Apollo, the legendary Harlem theater where I was something less than an overnight sensation. Timmy Rogers, an old vaudeville man on the same bill, explained it loud and clear: Harlem audiences did not care one bit that I was a promising kid-beginner singing "downtown" songs. Up there on 125th Street they expected a professional performance and tunes that were on *Their Hit Parade*.

We went to Washington for a week and then to a Rhode Island booking in Providence. Then suddenly there was no work—they were calling it the doldrums of 1938—and we went back to Chicago to the Oriental

Theatre. I had turned thirteen, and I was listening to words like "What this act needs is . . ." and "What that finale oughta have . . ." and I told myself that what the act really needed was a rest. At the end of the week I packed my suitcase and asked for carfare and a few extra dollars. I went home to Danville to finish high school, to pick up a local radio date now and then.

Everything was bad at home as the Depression continued. Reg was married and living in Evanston, just north of Chicago; Mildred had been deserted by her husband, and a second baby was on the way. We were facing eviction from the house Mother loved so much.

Over in Calumet City there was a club called the Caliente, and they wanted someone to play weekends: twenty-five dollars for two nights. In my tattered and outgrown white tails I went to work when the school week ended, and business zoomed from fair to good to great. Soon I could afford my first tuxedo. Then a fellow scouting talent in Calumet showed up. He introduced himself as Phil Shelley and said he handled Maurice Rocco, the popular boogie-woogie pianist. He thought he could get work for me, and he didn't understand why I wanted to go on with my education. "What do you need college for, with your talent?" He had booked Maurice Rocco in the Capitol Lounge, one of the hottest spots in Chicago. He was sure he could get me in there, too.

"Far from home . . ." Funny to be singing these words now, I know the Carlyle is home. My friends are at every table in the club. What enthusiasm tonight and familiar faces. There's Josephine Premice and her daughter, Susan. Nothing can make you feel an age—and by that I mean to feel older—than seeing the offspring of one of your close friends all grown up, poised and sophisticated.

She is sleek as any model, tall and thin—and a knockout, with humor and the darkest, brightest eyes that twinkle with affection and laughter. Like her mama, I realize.

This child is now a television producer in Los Angeles. I try to picture her at meetings, Susan an executive with the grownups. Probably just as cool as I saw myself at sixteen, with high school behind me. I followed my Pied Piper, Phil Shelley, to Chicago—and entered the world of the adults.

Chicago
1942

t was a three-shirt day in July, one of those Chicago days when every other hour you wanted to change not only your shirt, but every stitch you were wearing. At noontime I rode the el to the Loop from Evanston, where I was staying with my brother Reginald and his wife. On State Street the movie houses advertised "Sensibly Air-Cooled." The difference between the temperature on the street and a dark theater was enough to leave you with near pneumonia. I was on my way to the Capitol Lounge. I did not expect to see anything that was unusual, but I was going to be getting seventy bucks a week. A look at the place before I opened seemed in order. And it was nothing extraordinary, unless you were a guy out on a date or out looking for one. Then you had choices. Out of the Capitol and on to the next saloon, where the music might be louder and the lights gaudier—then to the next, where you might see more girls, and a next and a next.

State Street boasted live jazz in all the joints, though farther up the block from the Capitol Lounge the Rhumba Casino offered a glamorous girl singer and a chance to dance to South American music. I remembered that it used to be the Three Deuces, where only a few years ago Bookie Levin had taken me to hear the legendary pianist Cleo Brown and, when I had just turned twelve, my first chance to hear Art Tatum.

Though it was only lunchtime, the Capitol Lounge was fairly full. The friendly bartender gave me advice, glad to show a new kid the ropes, I supposed. A long bar ran the length of the narrow room, and near the front was the "26" table, where a pretty girl sat ready to roll the dice with the first willing customer; on the inside of the bar rose a platform, on it a piano and other instruments. I'd be up there working in a few nights—between sets, my new friend the bartender told me, I'd exit through a hole in the

Preceding page: Just before my eighteenth birthday in 1942.   21 floor to the cellar, where there was a room for the performers when they were not on the stand. The place was not as dingy as most because they stayed open all day and night, I guessed. There was the unsubtle glare of bright light that was exactly what the law allowed, the usual cocktail bar decor with the familiar Leatherette banquettes stained with liquor and cigarette burns. Lounge Moderne, I called it.

Down a tiny alleyway was the Chicago Theatre, the pride of the Balaban and Katz movie-vaudeville chain. I knew the block well because I'd made the rounds only a few years ago in those early days with Bookie Levin. Doors had been closed back then, but now I had a musicians union card in my wallet—Danville Local 90—and a contract for two weeks at the Capitol with options. And at that moment I wanted nothing more than to ride back to Evanston and get out of my sweaty clothes.

I was replacing Maurice Rocco, the talented black man who sang, danced, and played the piano with a dynamic left hand, all the while wildly tossing his long, straightened black hair as he stood through his entire act. Rocco was headed for bigger and better things, they were saying—"they" being Bookie and Phil Shelley, who were to split my commission on this gig and thought I was sure to follow in Rocco's golden footsteps.

My brother Reginald proved what a great fan he was when he refused to be cowed by the possibility of being turned away on my opening night. I was back in Chicago and he was not to be left out, unless there was a color-caused scene. A few old pals, all white, from Danville were there to join him—plus a healthy rooting squadron from the Club Caliente headed by my biggest fan there, Joe White, who'd taken me to the Capitol a few months earlier. The question of color never came up.

The continuous entertainment in their bars advertised by the partners, Greenfield and Schwartz, gave the customers at the Capitol more than their money's worth. Walter Fuller, who had played with the Earl Hines Orchestra for years, had organized his own small combo. Hearing him belt "Rosetta" was an absolute killer— "Rosetta, my Rosetta, never leave me for somebody new. You made my whole life a dream, I hope you'll make it come true— please do. . . ." I followed Walter Fuller, and I had no wish to emulate Maurice Rocco. I sang and played ballads, lots of quiet songs, and when the crowd roared for the boogie-woogie that was the rage at the time, I offered them "Yancey Special," something devised by James Yancey, a famous old black pianist, that was very popular. No master of the boogie sound like Yancey or Pine Top Smith, I admired boogie-woogie, but it was not what I did best. No matter—that first night most of the audience had been on a day-long bender; all they cared about was beat and volume. Volume came easy—speakers were everywhere—and after Walter Fuller set the pace, I had the edge simply by contrast. The act worked well through five sets, and at three in the morning I was back on State Street, on the way to the el and home to sleep.

During the next few weeks I realized that without some kind of contact, some form of exchange other than shouts and flamboyant gestures, I was never going to capture my audience. But there was also the glaring reality that for the most part the paying customers at the place were faceless, and that looking up from the narrow bar to watch a performer was only a short pause on an endless ride they were taking to nowhere—liquor was the message of the day. How to make contact, to find a style—that was the question I kept asking myself.

I was hearing great sounds from good musicians—at the theater next door, Harry James was playing and everyone was talking about his vocalist—the skinny Sinatra fellow. Across the street at Elmer's, the small, square-shaped room was featuring a young colored girl at a Gulbransen spinet, and along with her own inventions she was playing every Art Tatum arrangement I had ever heard—flawlessly. Dorothy Donegan was incredible. We met, discovered we were the same age—within a few months—and became good friends. I heard Sinatra sing that week, and later I was told that he stood at the back door one night listening to me and had said nice things. A white trumpeter named Wild Bill Davison replaced Walter Fuller, and his Dixieland was amazing. I was learning, trying to play new songs, singing them in a new way— finding new things to make those blank faces standing at the bar night after night focus on me.

It was a sweltering summer. One morning the phone rang in Evanston—Bookie was telling me not to come into town. A minor had been served an alcoholic drink at one of the Greenfield-Schwartz bars, and the Capitol Lounge was shut down. The partners had lost their liquor license.

The Capitol Lounge and the other Greenfield-Schwartz establishments were small potatoes in the whopping expanse of Chicago's bars and grills, all of them doing business. There was not a serviceman in Illinois—in the entire country, I suppose—who was not out for a good time. The bars opened as early as noon and did not close until four or five in the morning.

Only a few days later Bookie Levin was preening—he had found another booking for me. Phil Shelley had been a thorn in his side, the intruder Bookie had been forced to share a commission with. Now Bookie once again had proved his worth. After all, who had discovered me in Danville when I was six years old? Over the years the age of my discovery diminished as Bookie went on bragging—from ten to nine to eight and now as low as six. He conveniently forgot that my mother signed that contract with him and Leonard Rosen when I was about to turn twelve. Now I was going on eighteen—and opening at the Club Silhouette—on Howard Street, the last street on the North Side within Chicago's city limits.

Those sidewalks were a blur of summer khaki and white, with sailors and soldiers roaming the street day and night, a hum from the crowds moving with a genuine beat—that was one swinging street. Evanston, Lake Forest, Skokie, were all dry towns—probably because of Northwestern University and the Great Lakes Naval Station and the WCTU. When the folks from the north shore came south, they flocked to Howard Street, lured by the lights and the hot music. One thing was certain: they meant business—to make a little whoopee—have a barrel of fun—FUN in capital letters.

There was a war on. The draft was getting all the young men. Music blared out from every saloon, every bar. Neon lights flashed at intervals in counterpoint to the bright bulbs paving every theater marquee. Even in broad daylight the pounding rhythm of a piano came from one joint or another—from all of them at once.

Bars and saloons were doing capacity business. Grab a good time, was the feeling, and anyone could pick from one of the dozen or more lounges and bars lining the street from the old el all the way east to Lake Michigan.

Smack in the middle of the melee was the Silhouette, one more long bar that jutted out in a semicircle at its center with a stage behind it. Commonplace atmosphere with high ceilings, low lights, and no distinctive decor—not even moderne. If your performance surmounted the barrier of the bar crowd, you had a fighting chance with the customers seated at tables, customers there more for the drinks or booze than for the entertainment. I was at the piano in my summer jackets, and we were still living through the hot three-shirt days. But I saw warm smiles and friendly faces, and I was getting no persistent demands for boogie-woogie. I was holding my audience, and business was good. The friendly bartender made it a habit to slip me a rum and Coke after my final set.

Down the street from the Silhouette was a club owned by a formidable woman called "Killer" Kane. Playing there was Martha Davis, an all-smiles and glowing woman whose schedule was as wicked as mine. Killer Kane earned her name by putting despotic pressure on her performers, starting off with notions about proper dress and moving on to generous advice about style and performing. Martha had Killer's number from the start, catching her disapproving eye as Mrs. Kane looked at the short skirt Martha wore one night when she came to work. Before the boss had a chance to complain, Martha slipped into the ladies' room and emerged in evening dress. After work Martha and I would walk to the el, climb the stairs to the stuffy station, and wait for our train to Evanston, where we took a jitney cab the rest of the way home, since she lived only a few blocks from me.

Years later Martha married her bass player and called her act Martha Davis and Spouse. Working prestige rooms, she became a really funny performer in the style of Fats Waller. At one point she was represented by Phil Shelley, who was alarmed to hear that she was married. "She might get pregnant," he said. Martha laughed when I told her—"You tell him I'm working very hard on that right now!"

Johnny Mae was the ladies' room attendant, bright and a marvelous talker. A black lady who exchanged thoughts with me when we sat together between my sets, she sprinkled her speech generously with words you didn't associate with a woman in her position. We talked about the war, the state of the world, music—

and Johnny Mae carried on at length about her lady customers. I never discussed her status at the club, whether she worked for the owners or rented her concession.

Every night there was Johnny Mae in her black dress with narrow white lace collar and cuffs, her black bag crammed with hand lotion, toilet water, needle and thread, and whatever other articles were necessary to assist women out for a night on the town. And hand towels—Johnny Mae was careful about her hand towels—should a lady guest use one and then forget to leave a proper tip, she was not shy about letting the customer know that Johnny Mae was not in the ladies' room business for her health. Usually she began with a clearing of the throat—sometimes a few polite words. Then, if Madame

With Martha Davis on Chicago's Howard Street.

ignored these subtleties, she'd lash out. She took enormous pride in one such dressing-down, delivered as a young woman was headed for the door after using a hand towel without leaving the customary quarter.

"Twenty-five cents, please," Johnny Mae said. "That will be twenty-five cents, madame." And as the astonished customer expressed her surprise, Johnny Mae went on: "Just put the quarter in the dish there, Miss Bitch, and don't give me no shit because you *know* yo' ass belong to me!"

I have no idea how often over the past twenty-five years the murals on these Cafe Carlyle walls have been retouched. The delicate pastel tones may have faded since Marcel Vertes painted them back in the forties, but the charm of his witty brush survives, stylish, full of fantasy, and typically Parisian.

Did I know when I was booked into the new place in Chicago that it might have been named for the Dome, the Montparnasse cafe that was a Paris landmark in the twenties? But no writers and painters were hanging out at the Dome in Chicago. No Picasso or Braque came sauntering through the revolving door from Randolph Street in 1942. A street entrance was important to the psychology of the drinking public—a man in search of a cocktail was more likely to stroll into a bar from the sidewalk than to brave elevators and corridors, obstacles in the path to satisfying his thirst.

Against the nineteenth-century sobriety of the old Sherman House, the new Chicago Dome was rather startling, sleek and modern and quite Bauhaus in style. Polished steel framed the entrance and the interior as well. The use of minimal color must have been an innovation—walls and upholstery in gray and beige. The furnishings of polished chrome, the art deco that so appealed to saloon keepers back then. Simple, easy to care for—those lounge tables just big enough for three drinks and an ashtray. Fifty years later these details have not changed much at all, only the ashtray has had a noticeable decline. Above the curving bar was the stage covered by an ivory metallic semicircular curtain. What a glamorous room, I thought.

As it turned out, the glamour was not nearly as compelling as the family atmosphere that quickly evolved backstage at the Dome. And out front too something wonderful happened—it is happening again. Now I see the dear, familiar face at the table nearest to the piano—even in the dark I know the twinkle below the blond bangs. Jean Bach's loving eyes light up the room tonight the way they did at the Dome way back then in Chicago.

The Dome
Chicago
1942

rnie Byfield was a Chicago legend. Besides the Sherman, he owned the Ambassador East and the Ambassador West, where the Pump Room was one of the most famous restaurants in America. The name *Byfield* represented elegance in Chicago. At the Sherman his staff wore morning coats and striped trousers by day, tuxedos after dark. A string quartet could be heard as tea was poured every afternoon in a luxurious room off the lobby. Downstairs at the Panther Room, a name band was always playing. Other entertainment came from the Balinese Room, a spot for exotic dining with service by—as the ads boasted—real Balinese maidens. This supposed "authentic" touch was sometimes questioned by a knowing patron who deduced that the pretty maidens were from Chicago's South Side—and who just might crack up one of them with a few words of current colored lingo. Then there was the College Inn, famous for radio broadcasts by its headliners, the most important orchestras in the country— Duke Ellington, Gene Krupa, Jan Savitt, Fats Waller.

Now Ernie Byfield was opening the new intimate club he called the Dome.

Anxiety, stage fright vanished as soon as I walked into the backstage entrance the first night. In a minute the formalities of introduction were over, and I knew I was with friends—warm, gentle, and funny people. Sidney Pritikin played the accordion as half of a duo with a fellow named Vince Geraci, who played guitar, a "strolling" act, moved around the stage as Sidney did his fox-trot and they played their "society" music. That meant a mix of Gershwin and Kern, with a rumba thrown in for good measure. Then came their crowning glory: the appearance of a lively, lovely singer named Betsy Holland.

Sidney's wife, Evelyn, often came by with her mother and

how these two very bright women loved to talk! Peppy discussions took place; they could take a song apart and analyze it for good points and bad. Very sophisticated conversations, I thought. At seventeen, how else could I feel? There was harmony behind the stage at the Dome, with no questions raised about racial differences except for the recognition of foolish existing problems for Jews and Negroes outside our little world.

I was wearing my hair straight, and one evening Betsy Holland, giggling furiously, brought me a sandwich from the coffee shop—*where I was not permitted to sit*—a hot liverwurst-and-bacon concoction I had read about. "The girl at the counter thought this must be for the Indian boy working in the Dome. She said, 'Those people eat such funny food.'" This Indian boy thought the sandwich was delicious.

Aside from the coffee shop, no overt rules barred me from any place in the hotel. An occasional stroll through the Dome when I was not working, or a stop downstairs in the Panther Room to hear the band play a few numbers, was not off-limits.

From the spinet I pounded out songs like "Mister Five by Five" and "Tuxedo Junction." Betsy Holland and I did an "exchange" on "You Stepped Out of a Dream"—she sang a few lines and then I sang—and I had learned a few Cole Porter songs from *Let's Face It*. Sidney and Vince performed old show tunes from the twenties and earlier, and sometimes Betsy and I improvised when she mouthed the words at the microphone while I actually sang off stage. I'd guess we enjoyed that more than the audience—but it did work, and all our teamwork not only satisfied the crowds at the Dome, but the management liked it, too.

Alvino Rey, the master of the electric guitar, had won me over on the radio the year before, and he was supported by a group of top-notch musicians with swinging arrangements when I went downstairs to the Panther Room. To hear Yvonne King sign off with "Nighty Night" at the end of the Rey broadcast had been a special treat on the air. Now Yvonne and her three sisters, great looking and with incomparable harmony, were appearing.

I had had little or no exchange with anyone at the Panther Room until then—and no one from downstairs ever came up to the Dome to see any of us. Then two visitors appeared one night at our stage door, elegant young ladies, both of them. I was introduced to Betty Mae Nelson, a traveling secretary with the Rey Orchestra, and to Jean Ensinger Cherock, wife of the lead trumpeter. Jean was a Chicagoan who before her marriage had graduated from Vassar and pursued a brief career in journalism. She had an uncommon knowledge of jazz.

We discovered our mutual admiration—more like absolute adoration—for Ivie Anderson, Duke Ellington's vocalist for more than twelve years. And hearing Jean Cherock mimic an entire saxophone solo from an Ellington record made her close to immortal in my eyes.

Like the King Sisters, Betty Mae Nelson hailed from Utah. In minutes—seconds, really—we were babbling as though we had been friends for years. A few nights later Jean and Betty Mae came back with another member of the Rey company, an arranger named Jerry Feldman. Alvino Rey and all four King girls—one of them Mrs. Rey—found the Dome a refuge before their stint was over.

In that crowded room behind the stage of the Dome we used to talk about everything, and I did quite a lot of listening. Rosie the Riveter was going to receive pay equal to her male counterpart, and Eisenhower was leading an army into North Africa. We were all humming "White Christmas," and Evelyn Pritikin was as excited about some ballet music called "Rodeo" by somebody named Aaron Copland as she was about the Russians defeating the Germans at Stalingrad. And I was excited to hear that one of Jean Cherock's friends was the formidable jazz critic Harry Lim.

The ten-week run at the Sherman went through Christmas,

and I felt like a forlorn little boy when it came time to say good-bye to those new, good friends? Some paths separate, and people we are fond of vanish from our lives. Others constantly cross or run parallel, the good friends who remain good friends. Has there been an opening night in these twenty-five years when Jean Cherock Bach has not been at the Carlyle? How many times I have marveled at Betty Mae Nelson, treasured through the decades since as the legendary Portia Nelson.

What splendid camaraderie there was; no wonder my memory of the Dome is clear and cherished. It was easy to make up for the din facing us on a night when the curtains were flung back and we did our best to conquer an inattentive crowd, drinking and noisy. When some deeply interested patron found his way back to our inner sanctum and joined our discussions, he or she was made more than welcome. I had never had a better time in my life.

Take my five dollars . . . " I'm not one of
those performers who take the most innocent sentence
and turn it into a song cue. However, tonight the reverse
is happening—every lyric is not only reminding me of
something, but in vivid detail.

"Take my coats and collars . . ." I cannot remember
a time when everyone in my family was not tuned in to
clothes: my brothers, my sisters, especially my parents. I
used to wait for Papa at the train station for one of his
twice-a-year visits, and I was as excited about what he
might be wearing as I was about seeing him.

"And I've got ambition—debts beyond endur-
ance . . ." How did they ever manage sartorial style on
such slender means? "Two coats and collars . . . Pa and
Grandpa wore 'em . . ." He stepped off that train in a
proper suit and tie, overcoat, scarf, and a hat—nothing
I had seen him wearing the winter before. And polished
shoes, always polished shoes.

"Take my heart that hollers . . . everything I've got
belongs to you. . . ." Yes, the old adage about the shirt
off your back applied to my father. He brought me a
sweater, a tie, or socks, always something to wear.

Then there were my other idols, the movie stars in

37

the thirties who always seemed perfectly turned out. The individuality of Fred Astaire and Cary Grant impressed me. The tab on the lapel of Grant's tweed jacket that really buttoned when he put up his collar. Details like the necktie instead of a belt in the loops of Astaire's gray flannel trousers. Was anyone back then not impressed by the great Duke Ellington? And apropos of royalty, there was the unique look of David Windsor, the Prince of Wales, aka Edward VIII and then the Duke of Windsor—beyond style, the fit of his glen plaid suit, the cut of his dinner jacket.

One night in the fifties at the Cafe Gala, the glamorous Los Angeles club where I was literally everything from entertainer to checkroom entrepreneur, I took a topcoat from silent-screen star Buddy Rogers . . . a sensational beige cavalry twill single-breasted number. After I gave him his check and he went on to his table, I shrugged myself into it for a moment. It was huge on me, but never mind—I felt pretty grand. Fifteen years later I ordered my first cavalry twill suit from Sills of Cambridge—and I've been wearing cavalry twill ever since.

The difference between fashion and style is worth learning. Fashion is a follow-the-leader business, but style comes from you, how you see yourself . . . far beyond the reach of designers and magazine editors dictating what's "in" this season or the next. The dark blue suit, another in gray flannel, a tweed jacket or two, and a blazer—these get you through season after season and from town to town. And white shirts—or pale colored ones—pink, cream, blue, yellow.

Fred Astaire said he never wore a new suit until he had thrown it into a corner, stomped on it, and rolled it up in a ball. Because a man looked right when his suit looked lived-in—*bien culotté* is what the French call it.

American men long ago recognized that chic incorporates comfort; witness the seersucker suit. And you don't need me to talk about blue jeans.

What contemporary fellow didn't learn to break rules about dress after the sixties and the seventies? The turtleneck under the dinner jacket—no ties.

As a member of the Dukes of Swing back in Danville when I was in my early teens, I had a chance to take a firm stand about my own personal sense of style. A zoot suit was clown stuff to me. Those high-waisted trousers ballooning out at the knees and pegged in at the ankles, a gleaming watch chain looping down to slap against the thigh. And worn under an extra-long jacket with heavily padded shoulders. Then you added a rigidly blocked fedora with a brim so wide, a cord was attached to the jacket lapel in case of a high wind. Orange-tan shoes shined to perfection, a garish and very wide tie—big-city fashion, and the Dukes of Swing thought it the thing to wear for their first out-of-town engagement. Dark green zoot suits, pin-striped, at thirty-six bucks apiece and on sale right in Danville. I was the only holdout in the group—no way was I going to wear such flashy duds. Besides, I couldn't afford it. I wore my tight white tails instead, the suit I'd been wearing for years, each year outgrowing it more. The suit Bookie Levin had bought me for our first gig in Chicago.

THIS WEEK IN CLEVELAND

The Town in Review

Volume 11   December 26, 1942   Number 26

The Road:
Cleveland & Omaha
1943

am not sure what I wore for my first engagement at the Fenway Park Hotel in Cleveland; I clearly remember how I was dressed when I left.

Through the smoke-blurred nights riding the el back and forth from Evanston to Chicago, I had learned how crowded the saloon field was. It seemed to me that every available spot in the city had been turned into some kind of saloon, and singing pianists were a dime a dozen. More than that, I had the deep-seated feeling that I had not been reaching anyone in those boozy audiences. No great sense of security was evident in this train of thought.

Fortunately Bookie was oblivious of my worries and had not earned his nickname for nothing—after the Dome he got me gigs on the midwest circuit. The Congo Room of the Fenway Park Hotel in Cleveland, Ohio, is my most indelible memory.

Recalling my earlier days in Cleveland and an engagement at the old Hollenden Hotel, where I once had stayed, I found it quite natural to hail a cab when I walked out of the railroad station and headed directly for the Fenway. A friendly, smiling manager met me in the lobby—Mr. James Louis Smith—informing me politely that living quarters were not part of our agreement. Unperturbed, quite carefree—and young—I remembered a Negro hotel not too far away. I was on my way out the Fenway door, when one of the black employees in the lobby suggested that the new Cedar Street YMCA was close by.

In no time at all I was feeling completely at home in a clean and shining little room. And I was fulfilling a longtime fantasy—to stay at the Y meant a dormitory kind of life, part of my dream of college classrooms and amiable professors. The Cedar Y did not let me down.

Preceding page: Upscale advertising in Cleveland for the new kid in town.

43

I was the only performer at the Congo Room, and I found the living easy—after the initial shock of once again being billed as a specialist in boogie-woogie. This was a posh room, with no suggestion of anything to do with its African name: very small, with upholstered settees at the bar instead of stools and a spinet piano resting on a short platform, a microphone goose-necked over the top. There was a welcoming intimacy to the place, and I had to wonder how my predecessor, Mr. Kokomo, kept his boogie down to a roar in the miniature milieu.

No way to avoid contact with the customers in this kind of setting. Here was the chance I had been hoping for—an audience on comfortable seats close enough to the piano to reach out and touch—and certainly within speaking distance. What a contrast to Chicago, where I shouted to be heard on the other side of the room. I quickly found how positively intimacy can work—with an attentive audience and the challenge to live up to the expectations of a crowd of real listeners.

The well-heeled clientele at the Fenway were people of quiet sophistication. Cleveland's universities, museums, and symphony orchestra provided me with an education—so did the Cedar Y. I had only been out of high school for six months, and the fellows and girls I met, college-educated kids, were opening my eyes, making me aware of Negro history, theater, and art. Clifford Graves, an administrator at the Y, led me to the library. Relaxed, self-assured, correct, pipe in mouth, always wearing a tweed suit or a sport coat and flannels, Cliff introduced me to his wife, Marguerite, and they became mama and papa, brother and sister.

Four weeks flew by all too soon. The Cleveland job came to an end, and it was a success—but then it was time to pack the luggage and catch another train. Time to consider what came next. The repertoire had improved, a lot of useful experience had been gained performing in a small space, mingling with the customers when I was not at the piano. Catching on to saloon behavior.

Along with the new repertoire was a wardrobe—very different from the one I'd arrived with. The thought of buying a serious suit hadn't yet surfaced, but Cliff's influence was quite apparent—new tweed jackets, new gray flannels. The traditionally dressed college man. No, sir, I was not going to look like a run-of-the-mill saloon singer when I arrived in Omaha for my next gig.

Mrs. Sloan was a kind woman who owned her own house in the black section of town, and she showed me how to work out my transportation, getting downtown to Farnham Street and the Beachcomber. What a name for a club in landlocked Omaha. I was booked in for a month, four weeks—and there was never a rider about living arrangements in Bookie's contracts.

The Beachcomber was a cellar of considerable size—another bandstand within a square bar, this time a grand piano with lights above it. Tables a few feet away from the bar and a large square floor for dancing, which turned out to be a rare occurrence. Surprisingly, the Beachcomber customers came to listen. Except for the brightly lit performance space, this was the darkest room I'd ever worked in. With gracious owners, eager to be of help and, apparently, lovers of jazz who enjoyed the acts they booked as much as their customers. I was the "filler"—the act to round out or fill in the evening's entertainment while the star attraction was off. Jimmy Noone was the headliner—and I couldn't believe my luck. Noone was a fabulous clarinetist I had been listening to on the radio for years. A Negro well into his middle years, he now had reduced his sizable band to a simple quartet. At the piano was a pretty, smiling lady named Maida Roy, whose smart wardrobe and sleek hairdo suited the style and stature of Jimmy Noone's group.

The customers ate up whatever the Noone quartet played, from standards like "Sweet Lorraine" and "Mood Indigo" to a little waltz called "Japansy" that had to be a hangover from the twenties, when everyone seemed to be humming hit songs about the Orient. The owners were as pleased with Jimmy Noone as the customers, and I won their approval rather quickly, too. It was a completely comfortable job, and within a couple of days I was looking forward to my evenings at the Beachcomber.

The problem of how to present myself was still worrying me. In that appreciative atmosphere I thought of doing more than the current popular songs in my high school tenor. Even though my lack of years was shamelessly apparent on my face, I felt that for these sophisticated saloon hands something more grown-up was called for. Happily, it was not boogie-woogie these Nebraskans wanted—they were looking for melody and lyrics.

Except for the Omaha weeks with Jimmy Noone, I had never had a close encounter with high-caliber jazz musicians. It was a wonderful experience for me. But all too quickly we were saying good-bye with promises to be in touch, and after a day off I moved on to be filler-in for the King Cole Trio.

In high school in the Midwest the only chance to hear Nat Cole was on the radio—sometimes in transcriptions on national networks. My brother Bill, a big jazz fan, first heard the King Cole Trio singing "The River Sainte Marie" and made me listen, too. We were addicted—Nat Cole's own inventive, immaculate jazz style and smooth singing, the guitar of Oscar Moore, Wesley Prince on bass, sometimes the three of them singing together, all of it neat and shining as a new pin. Their small output of recordings had been trickling into the mainstream of the music business, and they were revered by jazz enthusiasts all over the country. By 1943 they had found a faithful following across the country, including Omaha.

They were relaxed and easy with me from the start. Nat was a fun-loving man with a sly sense of humor who appeared never to take anything too seriously. They seemed a loose, casual three-some—only later did I realize what effort produced that effortless perfection. No room for fluster, no time for anxiety—that was for beginners. Now on the brink of unprecedented success, they were relaxed—waiting for the good things to happen—and the eighteen-year-old bill filler, Bobby Short, saw to it that he was polite—playing the right chords and keeping his place.

Down in that cellar they were mesmerizing the audience, spellbinders in the dark basement. An open display of worship from women customers not very often seen. In those two weeks the audience hung on to every word—absolutely enthralled—and Nat Cole handled it all like the sophisticate he was.

My own reaction was not quite so sanguine after the Trio's second Saturday matinee performance. The Beachcomber had announced three o'clock shows, and the place filled up with avid female employees fresh from their downtown jobs. Throngs of young ladies lined the steps down to the cellar. Shopping bags, girl talk, and cocktails were the form. It was a sight to see and a great crowd to play for, until the moment I realized I did not see one black woman's face in the vast audience.

I had no idea of how many Negroes there were in Omaha, but the absence of any kind of racial tension was something I could not help noticing. One night at the Beachcomber a constant customer named William Sutton offered to drive me home after work. Bill knew a bar in the Negro section, near Mrs. Sloan's house. A music lover who had made friends with many musicians who came to town, he knew the saloon closed very late.

"How old are you, anyway?" he asked me after ordering drinks.

I admitted to my eighteen years, and Bill waited a beat and

then took another sip of his highball before going on. "How did you wind up in this part of town?"

Obviously it never entered Bill Sutton's mind that there were rules *and* difficulties for black performers traveling around the country. I told him I hardly had a choice; it was the only way for me to go. Not only in towns like Omaha, it was the same all over.

"Well, it seems to me you could have a room over at the Blackstone—a lotta performers stay there," he went on.

I was astonished—and I suppose I was complimented. Bill Sutton sized me up as suitable for the best hotel in town, the finest. To him the question of race was so much hogwash—something he never thought about until it was at his front door.

I really had found a friend in Nebraska. Bill and his fiancée, Suzy, took to showing me some of the loftier aspects of Omaha life. Blond and bright, Suzette Bradford was eager to learn and share Bill's jazz experiences, but she didn't like entering the lower depths of the Beachcomber unaccompanied or waiting at the front door when Bill was a few minutes late. Neither did other young women in Omaha—as the womenfolk began beating a trail to the Beachcomber to fall under the spell of Nat Cole, many upstanding citizens were wary and vocal. Along the lines of "Is it true *your* daughter was seen at that jazz place on Farnham, making a fool of herself over those colored entertainers?"

Bill and Suzy were my guiding lights and imperturbable pals. Quite often I went to Bill's house for dinner, served in what I presumed was English style—and once I was invited to visit Suzy's mother, who under glittering crystal chandeliers, on marble floors and rich Oriental rugs, presided over an opulent mansion, always with her ear trumpet poised not to miss a trick. *She* was not about to go down those stairs to the Beachcomber—but she did allow me to play her a few tunes on the family grand.

One night with Nat, Oscar, and their group I went to an after-hours club that boasted vintage jukebox recordings by Bessie Smith, one of Nat's favorites. Drinks were ordered, and several couples began to dance in the tiny space. A club employee was on the floor in seconds, his hand on the shoulder of Nat's guitarist, Oscar Moore, who was moving to the blues rhythm with one of the white women in the group.

"We don't allow any Negro men to dance with white women here," he said softly but firmly.

It was a reminder of the scandal in Cleveland only a few weeks before, black musicians and white women. I've forgotten the details, but there had been threats and orders to leave town— *or else*—those two words! The incident happened around the corner from the Fenway at a larger, noisier club. Bookie had told me about it, part of his guideline about what I was to expect and to stay away from when I came to Lake Erie. But by the time I got to Cleveland, the place had new acts coming in and there was a new black pianist pounding the keys, and the white women customers continued to shout for "more, more!"

So much for racial tension in old Omaha—to say nothing of forties Cleveland. Before I knew it, the time had come to pack up and move on. To cram my burgeoning wardrobe into my limited-space luggage. To spot a good-looking suitcase in a leather shop.

One of my Omaha fans had asked me to entertain at a Sunday night party. Cash never came up, but I assumed he would make arrangements to pay me later. I was chauffered to his house, played for his guests, and was returned home . . . with no mention of money, no request for a bill. His pleasant thanks at the door of his very lavish house somehow did not seem enough. This was a job of work for me and hardly a lark to play for people I barely knew on my one night off.

I saw the valise in the window the following morning. A few days later I realized I needed another bag. I called my erstwhile host, who obviously had no intention of paying me, and asked if I might borrow forty dollars. He was agreeable; a check would be waiting at his office.

The check was picked up, the valise was bought—the idea of paying him back never entered my mind. My one and only sting.

You oughta be in pictures . . ." I'm singing these words and laughing. "You're handsome as a Gable . . ."

And healthy as a Mix.
You surely should be able
To photograph like Richard Dix . . .

But never mind the laughter, these were my serious sentiments when I traveled across the country in 1943. To Hollywood. I had listened to Bookie Levin too many nights as a kid, to Len standing in the wings and urging me on. "Yeah, kid, you're gonna make it big." And making it meant only one thing—the movies. One place, one town. And I was heading for it.

"You oughta be in pictures . . ." I had watched the Nicholas Brothers dance in the Fox musicals. I had seen Lena Horne and Bill Robinson—if they made it, why couldn't I? I was convinced there was room for one more star out in far Hollywood. I couldn't think of anything else.

I had worked in Chicago since I was seventeen and in Peoria, St. Louis, and practically every small midwestern city before Omaha, before leaving for dream town. Everybody's ultimate fantasy, I suppose, and I felt mature and seasoned—even though twenty was still a while away.

California

1943

You're just a kid. We heard you were about forty and big and fat!" That was Harold Brown talking the night I went to look at the Radio Room, the club I was going to work at in Los Angeles. Harold was a handsome man with a wide-open smile, brown skin, and slicked-back hair. He played great piano, the kind that is the result of years of training. He held the crowd's attention from a stage opposite the bar. That was the largest room I'd ever had to play, but there was an easy atmosphere in the place. A fine sound system, chairs facing the piano—a lot of care to keep the customer's attention on the act. I had introduced myself when Harold finished playing.

"I know you're coming in tomorrow night," was his greeting. We sat at the bar and talked, friends instantly. His face fell when I told him I was staying at the Dunbar Hotel. "That's no place for a youngster like you. My wife and I have an extra room at our house—why don't you stick around until I finish my last set. We don't live far from the Dunbar, we can drive over."

Harold went back to the piano for his last set, and I was blown away by his jazz version of the "Habañera" from Bizet's *Carmen* that opened new musical vistas to me. After listening to his next two numbers, I knew he too was a great Art Tatum fan. Harold took his bows, and before leaving the stage, he went to the microphone.

"Ladies and gentlemen, I want you to meet the young fellow who'll be here in my place tomorrow night. He's from back east, and I'm sure you're all going to enjoy him—Mr. Bobby Short!"

I was surprised and took a quick bow. Here was an example of the thoughtfulness, kindness, and good breeding that made Harold Brown important among the jazz lovers of Southern California—that made him very important in my life.

Preceding page: The epitome of crew-cut cool in my gabardine and challis tie.

I knew what he had said about the Dunbar was quite true. I'd been briefed by the staff on the Union Pacific pullman coming in from Omaha.

Paul Lawrence Dunbar was a nineteenth-century black poet of note, but there was nothing very lyrical or poetic about the hotel named after him, nor in the neighborhood establishments named for other legendary black American entertainers—the Florence Mills Theatre, the Bill Robinson.

The Dunbar was a solid six-story building with a crowded lobby. Only that morning I had been aware of the noise and the hustle-bustle, all of it friendly, maybe too friendly. Not just show business people, but a sporting world as well. Gamblers, bookies—a lot of first-name and nickname calling. This kind of raffish crowd was hardly new to me, but I knew my mother would not have held with it at all. Surely not the atmosphere of the Midwest; nobody in Danville would approve. But the Dunbar was the best that could be had. Rich or poor, star or neophyte, adult or adolescent—if you were black, there was no other place to stay.

In the lobby I had recognized some faces from way back in my touring days with Bookie and Len—people from vaudeville, from the clubs. Faces I used to see when I stood in the wings, outside a stage door, or in an alley of another town.

Harold drove his perfectly-cared-for Olds through the late night traffic, pointing out a building of interest, a saloon, another watering hole that he had played. "You probably know my brother Lawrence, the trombonist with Duke," he said. Musicians and performers left out last names when they spoke about stars like Duke Ellington or Ethel Waters or Cab Calloway. Yes, I had heard of Lawrence Brown; he was the genius of the Ellington brass section. Harold told me their father was a minister in the African Methodist Episcopal Church. That made another positive in my regard for him. The AME had been our church at home, and while

I saw that Harold was no religious crusader, the connection with the church made everything much more than okay. This far from Danville and the bosom of the family, meeting Harold Brown was an unexpected reward.

As was 789 Vernon Avenue, the Browns' modest bungalow, blue and white and immaculate.

And Mrs. Brown . . . lovely, with skin the color of a Georgia peach, silken black hair to her shoulders. She was wearing something loose and long as she came flying to the door to plant a warm kiss on Harold's mouth, then standing back modestly to be introduced to this newcomer at his side.

Nellie hesitated a second before she said it—but I was supposed to be fat—and older!

There was a fire in the fireplace, music from the radio, and a few friends enjoying a drink. Introductions all around, drinks poured, and presently Harold suggested that I play something on the piano, a baby grand at the end of the living room.

An important moment. The kid from back east—and the room was quiet as I went into the chorus of "The Man I Love." The sighs of approval were welcome—oh boy, were they welcome! Then Harold urged me on to "Body and Soul"—with those multiple key changes and tricky harmonics, the bane of many pianists more experienced than I. If I managed it, I'd have passed this friendly test with flying colors. I played it in D-flat, playing the complicated inner passages safely, and finished off with a flourish to a houseful of applause. Nellie was beaming when she asked if I knew her favorite, "Yesterdays." The Jerome Kern ballad was a favorite of mine, too, and to this day I can hear Nellie's low, husky voice—"The very fact that you knew it!"—her praise, her enthusiasm.

Then Harold chimed in. "Excuse me, Bobby, for getting you into this, but we hear so much about eastern musicians, and sometimes when they get here they can't play a damn thing."

Later, when we were in the car, Harold repeated his offer. "Nellie and I have the extra room—why not consider it?" I said I would. Indeed, by the time we pulled up in front of the Dunbar, I knew I was going to accept.

A week later I moved in.

Perhaps being aware of what a kid I was added to the Browns' affection for me. I found that a bit hard to accept; after all, I did act older than my age. But most teenagers think that anyway. I remembered my mother's advice: Don't be in a hurry to grow up, take each experience as it comes along and don't rush headlong into adulthood.

How do you keep from rushing when you're surrounded by what you're supposed to be avoiding? When you are playing at a club every night, meeting new people all the time, loving the cozy and easygoing way that Nellie Brown kept her house. She really looked after me, taking care of my clothes, changing the linen in my bedroom. It was obvious that Nellie had adapted her-

With Nellie Brown at one of the memorable parties chez Brown.

self to Harold's unorthodox routine a long time ago, and now I fit comfortably into his schedule. We were never up before eleven in the morning, and the coffee was always ready, the orange juice fresh-squeezed. We had our big meal at four in the afternoon, and then we were off to work. When we were through I drove home with Harold, sat down to another meal. Often on a night off we went to the prizefights. There at the noisy, crowded Coliseum I met Ivie Anderson. Ivie had been Duke Ellington's singer for years, the idol whom Jean Bach and I went on about for hours at a time. Not being with Ellington didn't seem to bother Ivie at all. Now she owned Ivie's Chicken Shack, the restaurant that was a popular meeting place for all the musicians and entertainers in town, the Negro upper crust, and many white fans who found her fried chicken as enticing as her songs. Ivie was dark and thin and stylish, and her sleek Cadillac became a welcome sight on many an afternoon when she drove up to the house to gossip with Nellie.

Playing hostess was a natural thing for Nellie. She had an open-spirited, casual way of entertaining. There was always more than enough to accommodate surprise extras at her dinner table, and she was a fabulous cook. That crowd of seasoned performers who appeared at the Browns' front door, usually without notice, were people I had read about, heard of, or seen in the movies—Herb Jeffries, Louise Beavers, Nellie Lutcher. And how delighted I was to be welcomed into their circle. Not one of them was ever patronizing. The reality of being in show business seemed to guarantee instant acceptance as an adult.

Nellie wanted no help getting her food on the dining room table for her parties. At one I remember she had trouble keeping her balance with the enormous platters of fried chicken: no apron over her black crepe de chine, her hair done up, the topknot leaning slightly to the side, and small beads of perspiration mingling with her opal necklace. She got the chicken on the table, went back to the kitchen for an enormous bowl of spaghetti, and made more trips for the potato salad, platters of deviled eggs, and olives and relishes.

Duty done, she joined the crowd gathered around the piano. A woman named Evelyn Royal had taken on the awesome task of singing while Art Tatum dodged, dipped, and curved in and out of keys and rhythms at the piano with the agility of an athlete. Here was the man who hated to talk about his music, who had told me, way back when in Chicago, that the piano played itself. In those days Art Tatum would rather talk about basketball and the Harlem Globe Trotters. The room was smoky, but the crowd was rapt except for an occasional whoop that rang out when Art accomplished some daring feat.

Sometimes Lawrence Brown, Rex Stewart, Johnny Hodges, even the Duke himself, were on hand, as well as lovely Kay Davis whose floating soprano had replaced Ivie Anderson's vocals with the orchestra. Pretty women in their best moved through the crowd, sometimes stopping to plant discreet kisses on their men.

Often Ruth Cage was in a corner, Ruth of the olive complexion and the freckle-covered high cheekbones, the thick black hair she wore like Margaret Sullavan. Ruth, who looked white enough to melt into any Anglo-Saxon Protestant crowd. Ruth, whom I was stuck on.

Nellie may have thought that one thing missing in my life was a group of friends my own age. In case I was ever invited to a proper kind of party, with a proper kind of crowd, she had even suggested that I buy a blue suit. What was improper about the crowd at her own house I could not possibly imagine, but I did not ask. So it might not have been as impromptu as Nellie made it seem when one of her friends appeared at the front door with a very good-looking young girl.

She was Ruth Cage, an English major at UCLA with ambitions to be a writer and a longing to move to New York. Her

Ruth Cage—my
first serious crush.

vocabulary and her warm voice, her vast knowledge of things literary, fascinated me. Listening to her made me want to read. She
loaned me Faulkner and Proust and whatever current books she
loved. She was mad about music, too—and, of course, we became
great friends. Now I had a date with someone near my own age—
that pleased Nellie Brown almost as much as it did me. Ruth's people were not rich, but they were comfortable, with a house not
very far from Nellie and Harold.

No one went near Nellie's buffet until Art Tatum had swal-
lowed his last beer and was away from the keys. Then like locusts
the crowd descended on Nellie's table and silence took over as we

looked for places to squat and feed our hungry faces. Some of us settled on the porch or the lawn. What a surprise to see daylight—eerie to be out there among the oleander bushes, balancing a plate with one hand, eating with the other, and keeping an eye on the drink you'd parked on a railing or the grass. It was eight in the morning—the old streetcar came rumbling along Vernon Avenue, the eyes of the early morning folks on their way to work riveted by the scene on the Browns' narrow lawn—eating, drinking, laughing people greeting a new day in their party clothes.

Ruth looked at her watch. If she rushed, she could still make her first class at UCLA. I walked her down the few blocks to her family's house, past the large schoolyard and the empty lots. On the front stoop I kissed her good morning and went back to the Browns. Turning the corner, I heard the piano still being played, and I made out the tune—Art Tatum was wailing right into "Wee Baby Blues."

You take your date home, you give her an innocent kiss—rather an adolescent event, but instead of good night you are saying good morning and you have been at a party with the biggest names in jazz—legends, giants really—and you are accepted in that very worldly world.

Don't rush headlong, Mother had said, but how was I to avoid it?

Everything went smoothly at the Radio Room—at first. I followed Mike Reilly and his band, a comedy act that went over big with their rendition of "The Music Goes 'Round and 'Round." The audience howled at their shenanigans, even when they threw flounders out into the crowd. Another comedy group replaced Reilly; this time smoke poured out of their top hats—it was really flour, and it left the stage in a pile of debris with soot covering the piano, the stage, and me. I had been wading through the muck for weeks, their zany slapstick growing wilder at each performance before I stepped on stage to get to the piano. I went to Arthur Lyons, who was one of the owners. "I can't go up there to work in that mess," I said, and politely asked if some of the band members could help clean up their own litter.

"Mess or no mess, you get up there and work, Bobby, or you can leave right now."

I was making $150 a week, doing pretty well. Arthur Lyons did not care one bit what my space looked like in spite of the fact that I had developed a following, filling the room with an enthusiastic crowd and quite a few celebrities who came in to hear me play.

Or leave right now, he had just said in a sneering tone. A warning—or a threat—and suddenly those four words sounded like the best advice the man could give me. Without another word I walked out of the Radio Room, straight out into the street, feeling better than I had in months. I hailed a taxi and went home.

Harold had been drafted; he was in the army at Fort Huachuca in Arizona, and Nellie was trying very hard to adjust to a new way of life—with her man away. I needed a break, and Nellie loved nothing better than listening to music played by our friends, a late night at a few of the after-hours bars, where the rhythm and smiles and cheer were helped along by a couple of drinks. It was that kind of night I needed after turning my back on Arthur Lyons. And, oddly enough, I felt absolutely on top of the world.

Those after-hours spots might not have seemed as cool and hip at eight or nine in the evening. I think it was the very idea of being out late that made them attractive. The kick was that we were being raffish, even behaving scandalously.

And how folks dressed in those days! Hats and gloves on the ladies, always jackets and ties for the gents. There was never a disturbance of any kind. All the places were against the law—I suppose that was why a high degree of propriety was observed.

I still remember the names of the men who dominated that scene—"Stuff" Crouch, "Black Dot" McGee, and Johnny Corniche. He was my favorite, an easygoing chap with a slow but caustic sense of humor. Johnny was usually good for a free drink or two when I was short of cash, which was quite often back then.

I met Charlie Parker at Corniche's place. I never had to worry about being alone once I walked in; friends I had seen at the Browns' house usually appeared at one of the joints. And that's what the after-hours spots were—joints, though some of them were put together quite stylishly, one done by a top Beverly Hills decorator, another owned by the bartender from the Dunbar Hotel. And the crowds who gathered in those places were a mixed bag, a motley group of Angelenos, jazz musicians, and actors. The movie people were eager to relax after a long night in the studios. Rich and not so well-to-do, black and white—all with a mutual passion. Love of what was poured in their glasses, the booze that was served until all hours of the morning. Times sure have changed. People did drink—way back then.

Herb Jeffries, Duke Ellington's great vocalist, whose big hit had been the song "Flamingo," owned a spot called, appropriately, the Black Flamingo. One early morning Herb asked me to sing. Feeling no pain after a few highballs, I was happy to oblige—until I got to the piano, found I could not focus, and concluded that booze and show business were incompatible. A lesson learned—I've never again had a drink when I knew I was going to work. Not ever.

But where was I going to work anyway back then, after my declaration of independence? Henry Miller was an agent at General Amusement Corporation who had faith—and imagination. A short, mustached, and dapper fellow, he ran around town determined to find gigs for me. He found them. In the San Fernando Valley, in Glendale, any place where I could earn enough to pay my bills and send the check home to Danville. Then another demon raised its ugly head: the California State Board of Equalization somehow discovered that a busboy in one of my spots was under age, and questions were asked about all of us working there. Of course, I was jailbait, still under legal age. So again I was out of work; there was no job in any bar.

But Henry discovered that if one performed on a floor or stage at some remove from the actual bar, it was quite okay—and there were no restrictions on private parties. I launched into a series of evenings in Pasadena, usually at the Valley Hunt Club.

It didn't enter my mind to leave Los Angeles. The beautiful weather, that scent of jasmine and honeysuckle in the air, the persistent thought that at any moment I might be "discovered" by a studio mogul, had me convinced that I had to stay on. But most important was that from the moment I had stepped off the train at Union Station, the night I'd met Nellie and Harold Brown, they had made me feel at home.

One morning Henry called to say that the Trocadero on the Sunset Strip had talent shows on Sundays and he thought I should try out there. Here was a spot where unheard-of talent had a chance to air their wares, and the club drew a big-time studio crowd— great careers had sprung from these evenings, most notably Mary Martin, who had landed on Broadway in Cole Porter's *Leave It to Me*. On Sunday I did an afternoon audition, and Henry had an offer for me to work the following Sunday night.

The Trocadero was a one-story deco building that looked like a movie set, with Greek pillars and papier-mâché palm trees, all gleaming white with low lighting—instant opulence adding up to one word: glamour. And I'd be performing on the floor as part of a show; the California State Board could not object. The Trocadero always had a star act, at that moment my old friend from Chicago, Dorothy Donegan, who had taken Los Angeles by storm with new slinky gowns, new red curls, and her dazzling piano playing. If this spot worked for me and the one night led to a further booking, I had to start planning what I'd do, just in case—and then on Monday Henry called: could I go on that night? Dorothy was sick—the star spot was vacant.

No need to think twice about it, and no time. Just fast fixes on material and what I'd wear. Nellie sprang into action, pressing a suit and extra shirts, going over my shoes, socks—preparing. I didn't own any orchestrations, the band at the Trocadero wasn't part of my act—so that put one problem out of the way. I was off to the Strip for a quick talk-through about lighting, to go over an introduction with the master of ceremonies—and I was on.

An odd feeling came over me after I got through the first show. I was in my own dressing room; wasn't that some sort of achievement? I took a taxi to the bus that got me home to tell Nellie every detail despite the very late hour, and then I went to bed.

Early the next day Henry was on the phone—Dorothy Donegan had a bad case of laryngitis, would I go on until she was better? She was living only a few blocks away, and I thought a call to ask how she was feeling was in order. Her mother answered the phone. Dorothy's throat was so bad, she couldn't speak, but, "Thank you, Bobby, for helping out," Mrs. Donegan said. "Dorothy really appreciates it."

It was ten days before she returned, and then, as the management had promised, I had a booking of my own. A canvas banner floated outside in the Sunset Boulevard breeze, announcing my name to all the passing traffic. It wasn't the instant stardom I'd dreamed of, but my audience widened, the notices were encouraging—and I found enduring friends in a new act on the bill. From New York came the Revuers: Betty Comden, Adolph Green, and Al Hammer, with lively skits and the eastern wit that had made them a sensation. The fourth member of their act had been Judy Holliday, who was to make a movie and had to leave the group. Off stage the atmosphere was fast, funny, and completely professional—and we forged a camaraderie that has lasted through the years.

Nothing can be all sunshine—a night came when the club's audience, usually attentive, gave me a startling surprise. In the pitch darkness before the spots came on, the chatter did not stop; in fact, it rose to a near roar, as though one excited talker gained confidence from another. I was practically petrified as I began—I knew it was out of the question to get up and walk off; this was too important a gig. I set my mind on the end of a song, then the next and the next—soon, I kept telling myself, soon this would be over and I'd be going out to the kitchen to my dressing room. Then, through the haze of smoke and the special lavender spot, a figure was coming toward me. I went on singing until I felt his hand on my shoulder. "Just a minute, son—" The man took the microphone and turned to the audience. He was obviously no stranger to the crowd; I heard scattered oohs and ahs and applause as he started to speak: "Ladies and gentlemen, would you be so kind as to stop whatever in hell you're out there jabbering about for a few minutes?" At last I heard silence. "This young fellow is doing the best he can to entertain us. Now all of us here are in show business. How about shutting up and allowing this lad to go through his act."

I heard applause, he went back to his table, and I wound up to a responsive audience. In a few minutes someone in the kitchen told me the man was William Gargan, the accomplished actor who played the tough gangster with a heart of gold in countless films of the forties. I was too shy to step out into the room to find him; instead I scribbled a note of thanks for a waiter to take to his table. I've never known if he got it, but I've never forgotten his kindness.

The next week a gossip column in one of the papers came out with the news about Dorothy's laryngitis. She had, it said, not been ill but had gone to San Francisco to be with her fiancé before he went overseas. This was followed by another item a few days later—the fiancé was already married, and his wife had been quick to give the columnist the story.

A voice keeps whispering roam, 'cause any place I hang my hat is home." As I move into the last line of the Johnny Mercer/Harold Arlen classic, I'm remembering the end of that first California sojourn— and what came after.

My old pal Bill Sutton thought he was funny, sending me a letter addressed to Private Bobby Short. But a week later another communiqué summoned Mr. Robert Short to the Selective Service office in Los Angeles. My brother Bill was already in the infantry, and Reg was a sailor, we didn't know where. My mother was the real worry. I was her chief source of income, and after her years of hard work she was content to stay at home.

The musicians in our crowd offered advice—how to apply for special services, what divisions needed musicians. As it happened, suggestions were superfluous. The bottom line was that the military wanted nothing to do with the allergies that had plagued me since I was a kid. I was turned down.

In the months that followed, I wandered. No place was home—and I may never have owned a hat—but how clearly I can see those train rides. The war was on, so it was not easy to fly anywhere. Military priorities made space hard to get, and traveling cost the earth. From the windows of the train the towns loomed up and trailed away like mirages.

What a long time ago—when Los Angeles led to Milwaukee, to St. Louis, to a slew of other half-forgotten show spots. And, at long last, to Manhattan.

New York

1945

My New York life began when I walked down East Fifty-fifth Street and stopped at a Manhattan town house that in the thirties had been converted into the cabaret that was the scene of Bessie Smith's last stand—the Kit Kat Club.

I remember stretching slightly to peer through a small pane of glass that was set high up on the front door of the legendary Blue Angel—and how surprised I was to realize that it was no reflection staring back at me. No, it was another pair of eyes looking at me with an instant glimmer of recognition. Immediately the door was flung open.

"My dear boy, when did you get to town? Don't you remember, in St. Louis—Anna's friend? I am Herbert Jacoby." All of this was said quickly and with genuine enthusiasm in a heavy French accent. And he did seem pleased to see me.

I had heard about Herbert Jacoby when I was working at the Chase Hotel. Anna was Anna Sosenko—mentor and manager of the celebrated Hildegarde. And how I respected both women. The performer with taste in music as faultless as her choice of clothes. Playing the piano and singing, wearing chic gowns. And her strong, wise manager, who had generously given me much good advice.

Bookie Levin had really scored when he'd booked me into the Chase. I'd heard how smart an establishment it was, and from the rousing reception after my first show I had evidently lived up to its reputation. When I stepped out for my second show, I spotted three figures at the entrance to the club: Harold Koplar, who owned the hotel; a short woman I did not recognize; and Hildegarde. Here was the biggest star on the cabaret circuit—billed as the Incomparable Hildegarde. She was appearing downstairs at the elegant Chase Club, playing to capacity

Preceding page: My billing at the Chase Hotel in St. Louis—just under Hildegarde, one of my idols.

73

crowds every night. I had collected her records for years, I'd been singing her theme song, "Darling, Je Vous Aime, Beaucoup," since I was a kid. After my final bow I was greeted by a pleased, broad smile from Mr. Koplar and a shower of praise from the two women, Hildegarde and the woman at her side—Anna Sosenko.

We were buddies from that night on. Anna would invite me to the light booth whenever I had the chance, and I saw the subtle effects she created to make Hildegarde's act the surefire wonder it was. A change of color, a change in the intensity of a spotlight—and Anna whispering, "Watch this effect." The mix of soft blue and lavender light heightened in a second. "The crowd's a little slow tonight, but look, see how Hildegarde grabs their interest." After she sang "The Last Time I Saw Paris" there was not a dry eye in the house.

One afternoon Anna asked if I'd heard of the Blue Angel. Of course I had, and she went on. Herbert Jacoby was a good friend, and she was going to call him, to tell him about me.

Almost a year later, playing at the Park Plaza, another of Harold Koplar's hotels, I was greeted by a tall man with an accent. "My name is Herbert Jacoby—Anna told me all about you—if you ever decide to come to New York . . ."

After our first meeting at the Blue Angel, it didn't take me long to realize that his staring through the window was just one evidence of Herbert Jacoby's famous anxiety attacks. Had the weather been warmer, he might have been on the sidewalk, pacing back and forth, ready to hustle any passersby into his emporium, the way a barker would at a carnival sideshow. But the evening was too cool for Jacoby to show that he was looking for customers.

He led me inside to the dark bar, to gleaming black patent-leather banquettes, and he offered me a steak sandwich, a drink, anything I wanted. After a glass of ice water was ordered, he asked if I would like to see part of the show already in progress in the inner room that was the club.

The matchbook cover on the table showed a winged blue angel holding a flaming candelabra, nothing at all to do with the old Dietrich movie. Yet the atmosphere was definitely European, and the sharp, stylized decor somehow seemed circa 1920s Berlin. The tiled floors were black, the chandeliers red crystal, and the curving staircase up to the lavatories was white, its newel post a stylized white horse.

The cherub holding the glowing candelabra floated above the tiny stage in the showroom, where a pretty girl with a small voice was singing "My Grandfather's Clock." Evelyn Knight had been described as singing on tiptoe, and though the room was not crowded, she was charming an audience of aficionados. The lights came on when she walked off the stage, and a trio continued with soft, easy jazz. Waiters brought checks or fresh rounds of drinks. Looking around the room, I realized that this—now—absolutely—was New York! The customers looked chic and sophisticated, the men in dark suits, the women in the smart, no-nonsense dresses of the war years with elegant furs thrown nonchalantly over the backs of the little rococo chairs.

"Well, young man," Jacoby said, leading me out to the bar, "what are your plans now that you're here in New York?" He fidgeted, his voice nasal and instantly serious.

I told him I was looking for work, since he had been encouraging when we met in St. Louis—

"Well, Mildred is coming in for a few weeks any day now, and we'll have Irene Bordoni, too. Do you think you'll be available to start in ten days?" He was making cat's cradles with his fingers. "Of course, we can't offer you a lot of money," he went on. "After all, you are new to New York, but we can showcase you here better than anyplace else in town." I gulped and said I was sure the salary part could be worked out. Of course it could.

The Blue Angel—and the Mildred he mentioned had to be Bailey—on the same bill with Mildred Bailey! It was a dream come true.

Miraculously, a few days after Jacoby's offer, as if he had just been waiting for the auspicious moment to appear—lo and behold, who arrived in New York but Bookie Levin!

He took me to lunch and agreed that, though a salary of $150 a week was not much for four weeks at the Blue Angel, it was more than worth it. He'd handle the contract. The decision was made, the deed was done. I was walking on air.

At Jacoby's suggestion I went to East Fifty-fifth Street a few times before opening. One evening in the glamorous low light of the bar, I found a group of four men surrounding Pearl Bailey. With her upswept hair and elegant dress, with her attentive escorts around her, she looked completely at home in Jacoby's posh surroundings. Astonishing, after what had so recently happened to me in St. Louis.

Even in New York in those days it was an uncommon sight to find a group of black people sitting in an East Side cabaret. Then, no city was without its unspoken "no blacks" rule, particularly when it came to eating and sleeping. I had heard of the archaic edicts that existed even up in Harlem. Despite the overwhelmingly black population, it was customary for a "Whites Only" sign to be put out by uptown businessmen. It was the patronage of the white tourists that they looked for—not only at the legendary Cotton Club, but in other establishments as well.

Downtown only a small number of dilapidated hotels along Broadway were known to accept the business of traveling black performers who might be in town for a gig. Aside from these itinerant troupers and a few prizefighters, I suppose black folks did not travel too much. Very simply, finding lodging was a major ordeal—unless they had friends to stay with in strange cities.

I remember a night when I was leaving the club at the Chase

Hotel in St. Louis, where I had met Anna Sosenko, where she had introduced me to Jacoby.

The required exit from the club for a black performer was the freight elevator—down to the service entrance leading out to the street. Why I never knew—except that it kept me out of sight of the guests as I left.

It was not that late when I finished my last set and stepped into the elevator, pressing the button for the basement. The car descended slowly, and I was used to that—but at basement level, when it stopped with a slight jolt, the iron grate door did not open. The next couple of hours were an eternity, with no response to my shouts and calls for help. I wondered if I'd have to spend the night on the floor of the freight elevator, waiting for the day guard to come to work—and where was the night guard, anyway? Pressing that button to release the outer door, pulling and pushing the door handle, turned out to be useless. And pressing the buttons to go back to one of the higher floors was an exercise in futility. I was trapped.

I knew there was a busy, buzzing life going on above me on every floor of the hotel, and there I was—looking out the small elevator window at the dimly lit and deserted basement vestibule. Again and again I pressed the button panel. Then at last there was a click, a deep, grunting sound, and a slight lurch—the elevator began to move as soon as I hit the button to take me back upstairs to the club, back to where I had started from hours before. Out I went as the elevator door slid open, quickly moving down the corridor to the main elevators—the guest elevators. Past a few people in the lobby—past the night clerks busy with their ledgers and their guest books—through the revolving door—past the doorman helping a late arrival with his baggage.

To get home. To sleep. To block out the nightmare and its ramifications—until the next morning, with the riot act read to me by the hotel manager. I had used the guest elevator. I had walked out the front door—I, a colored entertainer, had dared to break the unbreakable rules!

"Did you expect me to sleep on the floor of the elevator?" I asked, and walked out of the man's office.

Despite freight elevators and front elevators, service entrances and lobbies, when my engagement was finished at the Chase the management booked me into the lounge of the Forest Park, another of their St. Louis hotels.

The city was almost like home. Life there had taken on a new form, something that would never have happened if I had not been staying at Cleota Spotts's house, which was one of those ace-in-the-hole moves from the beginning—when I first came to town, when the clerk at the desk of the Chase excused himself so very politely after I asked if there was a reservation for me. In a flash he came back with Harold Koplar, who explained the rules of the hotel—oh, quite diplomatically, of course—but they were the same old rules. Very clearly there was no room for me at the hotel, no way that I could possibly stay there. But the Browns had given me the phone number of their uncle, the Reverend Russell Brown, and his wife, Floy. Even Nellie and Harold had anticipated the scene in the stylish hotel lobby, and when I called, Floy Brown said she had been expecting to hear from me—she knew of a lovely place for me to stay. With Cleota Spotts. An upstairs bedroom with a bath just down the hall in her three-story Victorian house. With a grand piano in the parlor. Cleota taught physical education at one of the two Negro high schools, and she had many friends—successful doctors and lawyers and teachers. Successful, but not welcome at a Koplar Hotel. I soon made up for that by playing at the Y, the two high schools, and at Pace College. And on a Sunday at the AME Church, where Russell Brown was pastor, I was called from the congregation to perform. I had to think quickly what to play—and after finishing "Deep Purple," I was greeted with murmurs of "Amen" from the gathering and the beaming faces of Russell and Floy Brown.

This was a new kind of celebrity for me. A story in the *St. Louis Star-Times* made it all happen. The colored folks knew I was there, and I think they were proud. Suddenly a social life began; Cleota's phone rang day and night. When I wasn't working we were off to parties, to one local function or another. Sumner High, where Cleota taught, reminded me of a sepia Danville High. At their concerts I heard the same old songs from the glee club, a little soprano who sang Victor Herbert, a young lady who played Chopin at the piano.

One morning over at Vashon, the other Negro high school, I was asked to perform. What instant intimacy, I thought, seeing a concert grand placed directly in front of the first row of seats instead of on the stage. I saw one young lady slumped on her seat only a few feet from me, wearing lots of makeup, plenty of jewelry, and a fur coat obviously borrowed from her mother. After the first few moments of my opening number she leaned toward her companion and in a stage whisper announced, "He sure ain't movin' me." It was rather a relief to go to work that night.

The small room at the Forest Park drew appreciative audiences, and I had more liberties—small ones. Before going on stage, I was allowed to meet friends out in the hallway leading into the lounge. Warmth and good wishes went hand in hand with the crowd that came to see me. And happy camaraderie was a ritual at the evening's end. This has always seemed a most satisfactory part of performing to me—the mingling of audience and performer after the show. On those late nights at the Forest Park this rite was acted out back in the hall. Sitting at tables in the room was still forbidden. But when I finished work my departure was easier and more dignified. The lounge was on the ground floor. No elevators, no back doors through the kitchen— I could walk through the lobby and out the front entrance.

erbert Jacoby seemed unconscious of any social problems connected with being a Negro. He had unbridled admiration and infinite respect for colored people, specifically those with whom he had business dealings. In spite of his haughty manner—and at times he could be more than arrogant—Jacoby simply did not acknowledge the existence of racial prejudice. And at the Blue Angel, it did not exist.

Jacoby came from a solidly middle-class Parisian background with an education in music and political science. At quite an early age, much to the chagrin of his family, he had moved into the supper club world, and he soon established himself with an enviable reputation as the impresario at Le Boeuf Sur le Toit. Since he hung out there every night of the week, the word was that one of the owners said, "You're here so often, you might as well work for us." Jacoby made Le Boeuf the most renowned club in Paris, featuring entertainers from all over the world, particularly the black Americans who were so popular in the thirties. Jimmy Daniels had his first great success there, as did Una Mae Carlisle. It was said at the time that Jacoby boasted of knowing more black performers than anyone else in Paris. When he headed for New York in the mid-thirties he introduced his casual and suave Continental fashion of presenting his players in a small cabaret he named Le Ruban Bleu, above an East Side restaurant called Theodore's. Eventually he moved on to open the Blue Angel with Max Gordon, impresario and proprietor of the Village Vanguard, a basement boîte in Greenwich Village that had survived the speakeasy days and where he introduced many acts that later found their way uptown.

Soft-spoken, gentle mannered, and as socially unbiased as Jacoby, Max was a spry little fellow whose consuming interest was entertainment and music.

No wonder Pearl Bailey was at home on the other side of the stage at the Angel. I was sure she had experienced more than her share of back elevators—and for me the Blue Angel was offering the same freedom to walk through a front door to get to work. More than that, it was an obvious move up on the ladder, entry into another world of performing.

It was spring of 1945, and the Angel represented the ultimate, the absolute peak in the jealously guarded milieu of pub-crawling Upper East Siders. Jacoby and Gordon rarely missed any opportunity to bring something deliciously different and exciting to their customers. They were like a pair of Barnums choosing talent for the tiny stage at the Blue Angel. And they knew it was an honor and a privilege for a performer to be selected for an engagement there.

I went over to Fifty-fifth Street one afternoon to run through my material for Jacoby, to accustom myself to the stage. He took a keen interest in every detail of any act going into the club, and his advice was always reliable. He was invariably right, even when he criticized a performer's hairdo or her clothes.

The dark blue suits the men wore when they performed was as much a uniform as the ubiquitous tuxedo elsewhere. I bought a new navy blazer with brass buttons. A white shirt with a spread collar, a solid black silk knit tie, and gray flannel trousers suited me fine. Jacoby agreed.

However, my songs were a different matter. Immediately the old Ethel Waters classic, "Harlem on My Mind," was rejected. I understood his reasons. Never mind that I knew from a Sheila Graham gossip column that it was one of Garbo's favorite songs, that she had requested it when she went to the clubs in London in the late thirties. It may have been favored by the famous recluse, but Herbert Jacoby said no. Ethel Waters had introduced the Irving Berlin number in *As Thousands Cheer*—the lyrics were the expressed yearning of a Harlem Negro while living in the lush and luxe atmosphere of Paris. Jacoby had heard too many black performers sing it year after year, and he had grown impatient with its message. Then I found out he felt the same way about "Hottentot Potentate," a song I was devoted to. But we finally worked out a set of numbers Jacoby considered perfect for his all-knowing clientele. Lord knows that audience had heard it all.

The few friends I had in New York came to opening night, and Bookie was on hand with a small party. The show consisted of four acts, and I was to open the evening. The comedian Eddie Mayehoff followed with his wildly funny antics lampooning the upper-middle-class businessman and life in the suburbs. Then came Bordoni and Mildred Bailey.

Herbert Jacoby announced my name, and I stepped onto the stage. To say I was greeted by wild applause is accurate—wild, but not much of it. There were not that many pals out there. And at the early hour of the first show, smart clubgoers were probably still at the theater or at dinner, waiting until later, for the more stylish time to catch the three-star acts. I did the songs I had planned with Jacoby, and the reception was luke-warm. I could see the faces out front—sure that they were wondering who this newcomer was—and what was so special. Everything I sang they had heard before and done much better. My twenty minutes went by, I jumped up to take a quick bow, and off I went. Polite applause brought me back for a second bow, and then I made a swift dash upstairs.

Down the hall from the ladies' and gents' rooms was the usual shambles awaiting the performer in any supper club, perhaps a bit cleaner. After all, for a spot whose style and elegance was well known, the strolling players coming in and out of the Blue Angel did deserve some kind of comfort. A few rooms—probably the servants' quarters back in the Victorian heyday of the house—were on the second floor and very small. Mayehoff, ready to go on, was pacing the floor. Doors were open, and Irene Bordoni was applying the final touches of makeup while her accompanist watched. In another room sat Mildred Bailey, fully dressed in front of an ancient vanity table, with her hands supporting her face as she peered into the mirror. Nobody had told me where I belonged in this space. Out of breath, perspiring, and not altogether joyous, I stood around, wondering where to go. Mildred Bailey seemed to awaken from her gaze in the mirror long enough to smile and ask me in. We shared the room for the next four weeks.

It did not take long for the good times to roll in those tiny dressing rooms upstairs. Listening to Irene Bordoni mimic Mildred Bailey's knockout closing number, "Lover, Come Back to Me," was an experience. With her heavy stock-in-trade French accent, she sang along as Mildred's voice came up the steps from the stage. "Ooh, lovair, lovair, come back to me. . . ." The best came when Mildred heard Bordoni and began to do her own French parody as Irene crooned a little known Cole Porter song that displayed her accent perfectly: "You Don't Know Par-ee . . ."

Two friends I had met in St. Louis offered to put me up while I was in the city. One difficulty—they lived on opposite sides of town. Max Gottschalk, an industrial designer, had come back to New York to resume his career after a stay in Missouri and had leased an apartment in the West Fifties, where his sofa was at my disposal. My architect buddy John Paxton Hunter had taken a floor-through in an East Twelfth Street town house. "Packy," with professional acumen, had torn down the walls, turning the space into an avant garde loft. And I found myself with two New York City addresses.

I loved riding the Fifth Avenue bus uptown to work; the open upper deck was as much fun as a ride on a ferris wheel. Or I'd taxi from the West Side over to the Blue Angel. Either route, I found myself looking forward to the evenings with my fellow performers on the second floor of the club.

I formed a simple routine without even being aware of it.

Every day I explored another museum, and I particularly enjoyed the Modern, where I discovered Kandinsky and colors that I loved, forms I wasn't at all sure I understood. And I admired Mondrian, whose primary colors and angular designs I recognized because of his influence on so many artists working downtown in the Village. I browsed in the terrific shops everywhere in the city, and on my nights off I hurried to Broadway to see a show, to see Katherine Dunham—another new experience, to watch theater and dance merge into a blazing, rhythmic, sexy performance—and the Club Zanzibar, where all the big-time Negro stars landed, where a chorus line of the best-looking girls danced for an integrated audience. Quite a change from the old Cotton Club days, where only the elite of Harlem were allowed in to see a show and then, I had heard, only on one night a week. Yes, New York was a revelation—after Dunham I found Martha Graham— with Aaron Copland's glorious music for "Appalachian Spring"—and Canada Lee doing Shakespeare, *The Tempest* with Vera Zorina: Canada Lee playing in whiteface at the same time Mary Martin was in rehearsal for *Lute Song* as a Chinese princess. And Betty Comden, Adolph Green, and Jerome Robbins had two colored performers in *On the Town*. This was a major innovation, a first time . . . well, there was Robbins's superb subway ballet in the show, and we did ride the subways, didn't we? At a newsstand I bought the newspaper *PM*—unlike any other paper, I'd been told, because of its liberal editorial policy. New York was an education as well as a revelation.

A big blessing in my big-city life was being adopted by Fredi Washington and her sister, Isabelle Powell. They lived on St. Nicholas Avenue, and after I was accustomed to the subway system, I visited them quite often, sometimes staying for dinner. Fredi and Isabelle treated me like family. Well, Fredi was practically family, I thought—Nellie Brown's sister-in-law, married to Harold's brother Lawrence, who was Duke Ellington's star trombonist. The marriage was not going well, but Fredi, who, after a great success in the movie *Imitation of Life*, found it hard to find work in Hollywood, was persevering. A fair-skinned beauty not about to "pass" and not in much demand at the studios, she had made a reputation on the Broadway stage. After appearing in *Mamba's Daughters* with Ethel Waters, she was reading *Lysistrata,* the classic drama slated for an all-black production the following season, and she wrote a column for a Harlem newspaper.

We laughed when I reminded her of a phone call to Nellie Brown back in California. Fredi had asked what they were having for their usual late night snack, and she was aghast when Nellie said they were eating creamed salmon and rice. "No wonder you guys are always complaining about your weight." This from Fredi, who hadn't gained a pound since the thirties.

Now these women had more serious things on their minds, but they showed me nothing but kindness and consideration. One evening I met them at Grand Central Station. Isabelle was on her way to Reno—to divorce Adam Clayton Powell II, the preacher from Harlem's Abyssinian Church, a representative in Congress, and one of the most important men of his race in the country. Here were the two beauties being escorted to a flower-banked drawing room on the *Twentieth Century*. The sisters were in their finest spring finery—Fredi in black and a silver fox jacket, her black felt beanie with a red rose tilted to just the right angle. I asked where Isabelle was going to be staying—out there in Nevada, in racist country. There was a Negro woman who took in lodgers, Fredi assured me.

I was reminded of the old days when finding a hotel, a clean one with a clean bed, was nearly impossible for a Negro on the road. I had some friends who once stayed in a place where their chambermaid had been an ex-vaudevillian, and when they were ready to check out, the woman, knowing they were in show business, presented them with a sheet she had filched from the hotel laundry supply. A useful gift to be given in difficult times. I could not help thinking of Nellie Brown, who was always aware of such situations. Nellie had "prepared" me—that was how she put it before I left California. A kid who was brought up in a family where the girls did the cooking and the household chores needed to be shown how to pan-broil a chop, to cook vegetables. And he should be able to iron his own shirts, to do his own laundry. Yes, Nellie knew, and indeed, she saw that I was prepared.

But standing there in Isabelle's drawing room on the *Twentieth Century,* I realized that Nevada landlady was never going to see a more glamorous boarder.

Over at the Blue Angel there would sometimes be a surprise in the audience. One night after I had been announced and was about to sit at the piano, I spotted an unmistakably familiar face at a front table: Clifton Webb, with his mother, Maybelle—as always. Before going into my first number, I smiled and said good evening. Webb flashed the haughty, recognizable look I knew from his movies, and as the eyebrows arched and the lips pursed he hissed, "What?"

I knew this was one hell of a way to start a night's work.

Bookie Levin came in and out of town quite often, sometimes coming up with an interesting offer for me. He called one day to announce that John Murray Anderson, the famous director of musical extravaganzas, was putting on a new revue. The auditions were being held at the Diamond Horseshoe, the famous West Side nightclub owned by the equally famous Billy Rose. Here was an exciting new prospect to think about, and when the day came I sat for an hour or so, watching other hopefuls sing, dance, and do acrobatics before a small panel of experts—the jury who made the decisions. They surrounded Anderson, a rather stout man with a slight English accent, who was as celebrated for his sharp tongue as he was for his talent—and for the nicknames he gave people he worked with. An actress whose figure was far more striking than her accomplishments he called "Total Waist." A brilliant designer he worked with was a bit wispy in personality, so Anderson called him "Spring." Irvin Graham, who had written songs for the revue *New Faces*, an elegantly dressed young fellow, was always called the "Rich Mr. Graham." And the producer Leonard Sillman was "Koko," apparently reminding Anderson of the *Mikado*. No explanation was needed when he named the leading ballerina the "Laundry Bag."

Before my turn, one of the members of the jury came around to talk with me. "You must be Bobby Short," he said. "I hear you sing and play little songs at the piano. You may certainly do something for us if you like, but frankly, there's no place in our plans for your kind of performance."

That was that. I headed for the street, hurt by the abrupt treatment. At least I was not going to be given a John Murray Anderson nickname. Maybe there was more than a bit of truth in what the fellow had just said. People who played and sang little songs were probably a dime a dozen in New York. And maybe playing and singing *little* songs was not all that it seemed to be. My first lesson. I knew I had more to learn. And a teacher appeared.

Don McCray always appeared from out of the blue when he was most needed. I met him when I was a kid in vaudeville, and then he had appeared one night at the Radio Room when he was working on the movie of *This Is the Army*. Don gave me good advice about hitting a high note with less effort, he recommended new music, and he made valid suggestions for my act. Now he had more sage advice—like going over to West Fifty-second Street to hear Mabel Mercer at Tony's.

In a rather faded room Mabel drew a packed house every night—prominent people from the theater and Hollywood, the fashion crowd mingling with faces from the society columns, all of them eager for her entrance through the narrow path between crowded tables to the thronelike chair in front of the piano. What a lesson to watch that entrance—her blue eyes glowing, her smile the smile of royalty. But there was no icy snobbism in her manner; this was a monarch adored by and adoring all her subjects. She sang in a high, floating soprano with faultless diction. I had known many of her songs for years, but watching her was a revelation. No worthwhile song from a Broadway musical escaped her; composers brought her new music, and never was a lyric sung with more understanding perfection. She sat on the chair and sang everything from heartbreaking ballads to light, witty numbers that made her audience respond with shared gentle laughter. And all of it was delivered in a voice that was barely stronger than someone chatting with her closest friend. The reaction was beyond friendly—it was more than affectionate—I was sure this was true love as the room filled with admiring sighs of "Oh, Mabel!" instead of applause.

It was a lesson to sit there and watch her—sometimes she left the platform to go to a table and sing a requested song to a totally entranced couple. This was Mabel Mercer's world, and how happy I was to be there.

When at last she had gone off, Tony, the owner of the club, rushed to her spot on the platform, and in a split second he was standing on his head. He got his laughs, and I wondered if he was jealous, relegated to the sidelines, anxious to get a round of applause for himself—a little acclaim for his shrewdness in giving the crowd the gift of Mabel Mercer.

Four weeks went by. My first show was cut short, and it was not easy going through those evenings when I thought the applause was never going to come at all. Yet no one seemed to be aware of the disappointing reception I was getting—not even Mildred or Irene Bordoni. Jacoby and Max Gordon remained helpful and encouraging, the way they had been from the start. One night before my first show Herbert Jacoby came over to me.

He said he had something on his mind, and I could tell it was something important. In a quiet and serious voice he spoke about his faith in my potential.

It took a lot of control not to say it out loud—"Potential!"—but I held my tongue. Maybe I had come to New York too soon, Jacoby was saying. What were my plans—did I intend to leave the East? He knew of a room up in Boston that drew quite a sophisticated clientele—it might be an opportunity to hone the act in another town. I was touched by his concern. Then a few nights later he had another suggestion. What about Montreal? He had a friend in town who booked a room up there.

I closed a few days later, just as the war in Europe ended. New York was more exciting than ever, the streets filled with thousands of people. Shouting, joyful crowds—caring, affectionate men and women, boys and girls—everyone sharing. Cheering. The thought of leaving the city was unbearable. Canada. In Montreal there was this club I had never heard of— the Cafe Samovar. What difference did that make? I had been playing in rooms that were unknown quantities to me for years.

Yes, I loved New York, but there was reason to doubt that New York was ready to love me.

My reception at the Blue Angel never rose above the polite applause of opening night. Somehow I got through those four weeks, and I guess I even won a few kudos along the way.

The truth was I had not lived up to Jacoby's expectations— or Anna Sosenko's. Or my own. I was devastated. The lady had been right when she said to me one day that not making it in New York was really the pits.

Sand in my shoes, sand from Havana,
Calling me to that ever so heavenly shore. . . .

As we move into the first few bars, there's that reward-
ing surge of satisfaction that comes from the crowd
when they recognize a familiar number. And I owe it all
to Maggie Long.

I'd been in and out of countless short gigs after my
less-than-startling entrance into Manhattan club life,
and one of them was a dismal engagement at Ping Bell's
Steak House in Phoenix. Arizona, that is. Ping looked a
lot like Paulette Goddard, and she didn't belong in the
prejudiced atmosphere of a town without a place for me
to stay, or eat. I had a four-week booking—after one
night, I gave her my two-week notice.

Maggie Long was a savvy New York model, in
Phoenix on a fashion shoot. She came into the bar one
night and introduced me to "Sand in My Shoes." I've
been singing it ever since. And blessing her every time.

Also often on hand were three air force officers from
nearby Williams Field—Mike Lanin, nephew of Lester,
the society-orchestra leader, and his two friends, Barney
Rosenblatt and Phil George. Those three, along with
Maggie, saved the day many a night.

Every song suggests someone, someplace—a street, a city, a special time of the year or time of day. When I finally arrived in Los Angeles, after what seemed an endless road tour, Doris Rhodes brought me another number that became a signature. Doris had made a country-wide reputation on the airwaves with her inimitable rendition of "Deep Purple." At the Cafe Gala, the smartest Los Angeles spot any performer could land in, she sang Yip Harburg's simple, sophisticated lyric for me.

I like the likes of you,
Your looks are pure deluxe,
Looks like I like the likes of you.

Did I like it? I've loved it—and used it to end almost every performance, ever since. All thanks to Doris.

California
1946–1952

There must have been plenty of sand to shake out of my shoes when I got back to Los Angeles after Phoenix. I was out of work, and I wasn't even liking the likes of me very much until the morning Phil Shelley came up with the idea that I might go into a place called the Haig on Monday nights when the regular pianist was off.

I had passed the ramshackle cabin on the bus going in and out of Hollywood. The Haig was smack in the center of the sleek Miracle Mile, but it could have been blown clear across the plains, Oz style, from Nantucket or someplace on Cape Cod.

The first Monday was meant to be nothing more than a way to earn pocket money, though getting inside the tumbledown and picturesque saloon did satisfy my curiosity. And it was a challenge to be working for a complete evening without singing a song. In 1946 a federal law had been passed that allowed a bar, any bar, to have a pianist playing for customers. However, if words were part of the performance, an entertainment tax had to be added to the customer's tab.

The owner's name was John Bennett. I think he opened the Haig in the first place just to have somewhere he could treat his friends to the music he most enjoyed.

I played it safe that first Monday, sticking to renditions of the songs I liked. For a long time I had been aware of the cool, laid-back style known as New York piano, best exemplified by the master of the trend, Cy Walter. I had seriously tried imitating the way he played the standards from "Star Dust" to "Body and Soul." Cole Porter's "Begin the Beguine" was now one of my songs, and I was also doing "I Can't Get Started" and "The Blue Room." John Bennett had been most attentive right up to the end of my first set—when he picked up his cigar from the ashtray and marched by the piano beckoning me to follow him to his office, where along one wall were row after row of shelves holding 78 RPM singles and stacks of albums. In a minute the room was filled with the music of the real Cy Walter, then some popular two-piano team, followed by Bud Freeman's saxophone interpretations of obscure Porter. Bennett took two minutes to find a match and relight his cigar, while I waited for the compliments I knew were coming my way for the perfect just-obscure-enough set of songs I'd just finished.

"What was that last number you did just now?" Bennett asked.

"You mean 'My Future Just Passed'?" I replied.

"Yeah, isn't that a Richard Whiting song?"

I got the idea. John Bennett was not to be put down; he was letting me know that *he* knew *his* music.

In truth, the place was nothing more than a neighborhood bar—but above all it was John Bennett's saloon. After closing, he bought me a nightcap and asked if I would like to come back the following week. Nothing else was going on for me—besides, I'd had a good time.

When I walked in the next Monday night I knew John had been spreading the news. He had made a "discovery," and he was going to run with his own optimism and excitement. The Haig was packed, and he knew every customer in the place. At the end of the evening once again he called me over to the bar. After a little preliminary hem and haw, he said he would have to give his regular pianist notice, but . . . well, would I be interested in a regular job? I had played in many oddball places since I was twelve years old, but never one like the Haig. How much was the job worth? John wanted to know. He had never hired someone like me—was it worth taking the chance? I thought it sure was and suggested that he talk to Phil Shelley first thing in the morning.

think it began back there at the Haig, seeing for the first time the importance of a personal following. Oh, I had garnered some fans in Southern California, but I had shared them with the headliner of the evening, the star of that particular gig. At the Haig, slowly but surely, I learned what I was in the overall scheme of this segment of showbiz. The intimate performer, sharing that intimacy with the crowd—and the crowd there at the Haig showed me what it was like to be on my own turf. It was a new direction—maybe the first real direction.

Talk about Joseph's coat—were there colors in that place night after night! From the reds and greens of the sporting world to the dark blue of business and the heathery tones of academic tweeds. I don't recall any deep purple for prostitution or gambling, but there were yellows and golds, rose and orange, many pastels for the innocence of the place. Again the old rule—the customers were a reflection of the owner's character. John's laissez-faire attitude was apparent everywhere in his saloon. Any business or behavior demanding more serious surroundings than the atmosphere he had created could better be transacted somewhere else. In his gray wrinkled flannels, his unpolished Weejuns, John moved in and out of the crowd, grinning his million-dollar grin, not even stopping to apologize for forgetting to place an order for bourbon that day.

I realized there was a group that could be called "regulars" coming in night after night. I loved looking at these remarkably attractive girls, underfed and slightly arrogant. Completely pulled-together creatures. Models who came in with the photographers they posed for. And artists fresh out of the Chouinard Institute, others who were designing or wanting to—most of them longing for New York. I became aware of these people because of their complete attention to my work and the way they looked, the way they dressed—oh boy, were they it! And they were my followers, my first real fans. Before long they were my chums, too.

I gained an appreciation and respect for drawing because my pals Pauline Annon, Fred Matthews, and Betty Brader worked for the best stores in town, their illustrations gracing ads in the papers and magazines. Erven Jourdan was a gifted photographer, his wife an artist, too. She did the illustration for my first record album. One day I went to a Maggie Teyte recital with Hollis Williams and his sister, Anita. There we heard the glorious English soprano sing songs by Debussy and Fauré, and I saw what total professionalism and expertise were required for a recital performance—Teyte, well into her sixties, was at the top of her form—the audience response was staggering.

Weeks stretched out to months, and business improved by the night. The news had spread—just a stone's throw from Wilshire Boulevard in a tumbledown saloon was music, East Side New York music. And I was playing a pretty good game imagining I was in New York. John kept the lights down low, while a pink spot flooded the piano. A faint aroma of expensive perfume was in the air. It lingers in my memory to this day, mixing with the heavy scent of cigarette smoke. Maybe it was not Manhattan—but, as I said, I was playing a pretty good game of make-believe.

The crowds grew larger. Going to the Haig was *the thing* to do. And, increasingly, I gave those crowds what they expected—crowd-pleasing music. That was how it was, I figured, the old tried-and-true big songs, the rousing openers, and the crash finishes.

On a Saturday night the place was packed, the front steps weighed down with customers waiting for the next show—I reached the end of the set with a big finish. And there was bigger applause. I gave them a specially deep bow and stopped at the bar for a few words with John. Cheerfully I asked how he liked seeing the room packed.

"Why in hell didn't you sing 'Deep in the Heart of Texas' and be done with it?" he snapped. He had no time for the cash register; I was breaking his unspoken rule by bowing to the demands of the public. "After all, I didn't really hire you for *them*, did I?"

John Bennett had made his point. A week later one of the new customers approached me: David Hanna, the drama critic from the *L.A. Daily News*. "Has no one written or done anything about your engagement here—like publicity?" he wanted to know. How good to hear something constructive instead of a few effusive adjectives when I stepped away from the piano. No, I told him, not a word, not even in the trades like the *Hollywood Reporter* or *Variety*. He called later in the week, asking for more pertinent facts, and a few days later a full column appeared in the *News* trumpeting what was happening out on Wilshire Boulevard because of Bobby Short.

John's reaction was ambivalent—surely somewhere deep down he had to be touched by and proud of such a paean for his protégé and the Haig. But, as his little shack became more and more popular, the overflow of new faces was clearly unsettling to the old-guard patrons—and perhaps to John himself. At twenty-one, how could I know that success constitutes a threat to the status quo?

After four months a leave of absence seemed in order, and John was more than agreeable. This was to be a pattern I was not yet aware of: a change of scene, a bit of a rest, and the chance to make a "triumphant return engagement." I was going off to New York, to look for new material and a few New York suits.

There were replacements for me at the Haig. The piano was never replaced. The beat-up grand lasted until the club closed.

Virginia Maison went on for me while I was in New York, a bubbly blonde who sang "Chichicastanango" faster than anybody else and also performed what was considered "risqué" material.

A few days before my return to the Haig, the phone rang early one morning. "Bobby, we've had a problem here with the vice squad," John was saying. "You know what they're like, they showed up one night and threatened to cut off my singing license if I didn't get rid of Virginia or get her not to sing at all. They'll be back for your opening, just checking, but lay off anything they might not know. It should be all right if you sing a lot of standards."

Fine, I thought. I had a great supply of standards, all the songs John Bennett hated hearing. On opening night he gave one of his supposedly subtle signals when two men arrived. Nondescript in tweed suits, they could have been any two guys out for a night on the town. A pleasant surge of déjà vu came over me as I launched into a parade of songs I hadn't played since I was a kid in Danville—"Basin Street," "St. Louis Blues," "Dinah." The rosy glow lasted until one of the regulars sitting up front shouted out, "What the hell's going on here, Bobby? Sing 'Experiment'!" This Cole Porter song was introduced by Gertrude Lawrence in a 1930s musical called *Nymph Errant*—one of the esoteric numbers a few saloon singers performed to the delight of the cognoscenti. The lyrics were innocent as could be—but might be construed by the unsophisticated as bawdy or too suggestive. I hesitated—but the customer was adamant, obviously bored with my renditions of the standards.

As I passed the bar John told me our special guests were waiting outside to talk to me. And an explanation of the lyrics was expected. It seemed the very title of the song had conjured up any number of possible sexual interpretations. Impossible, I told the two wide-eyes interrogators, didn't they realize the song was from a *British* musical and was written by Cole Porter?

"Cole Porter?" One of them looked at his cohort and then both of them, clearly puzzled, turned to me with, "Who's he?"

Performers were finding their way into the Haig after work downtown at the Biltmore Theatre or at the old Philharmonic. Between downtown Los Angeles and our street stood the Town House, a rather elegant little hotel preferred by many theater folk—and from there actors, musicians, and ballet dancers were showing up at the little shack on Wilshire. It occurred to me that New Yorkers felt exiled after only a few weeks, sometimes only a few days, in Los Angeles. Any saloon offering a New York kind of music satisfied their hunger—and thirst.

Ballet Theatre arrived in town, and two of the leading dancers found their way to John Bennett's door after a short wait on the rickety front steps: Muriel Bentley and John Kriza. Both were as winning in person as they were on stage—more so, because they shared a sense of humor and a nice, easygoing attitude. Ballet seemed to me a totally other world. But I had seen them dance *Fancy Free*, the Jerome Robbins–Leonard Bernstein ballet that led to the musical *On the Town*. They were great fans of Mabel Mercer. And at Muriel's request I added another song to my repertoire: "Remind Me," by Jerome Kern and Dorothy Fields, a number Mabel often did. Saloon singers used to have a slew of songs like "Remind Me" at their fingertips. The world-weary lyrics represented some kind of appealing bittersweet philosophy to that earlier-era nightclub crowd.

Fashions run in music as in everything else, even in the Haig days, but fashion was not what I was about. Style was my goal . . . and I'll be forever grateful for the guidance that came my way back then. John Bennett always had ideas about what I should be singing. The five-and-ten on Hollywood Boulevard still had a sheet music counter, and the lady in charge was more than willing to sit at the white baby grand and run off any tune. Somewhere behind her pleasant and made-up facade was one more frustrated performer. And downtown at Birkel-Richardson, my pal Al Hammer was the best at sight reading and proud of the secret goodies he stashed away for special clients—like me. I was learning by a process of assimilation—by osmosis.

By the spring of 1948 I felt restless. Five years earlier I had arrived on the West Coast. I had been playing in and out, off and on, ever since—the Radio Room, the Trocadero, out in the Valley. And now, quite happily, at the Haig. But voices inside me kept saying move along, push on.

I hadn't paid too much attention to the visits of Eadie Griffith and Rack Godwin to the Haig, not any more than I had when I saw John Walsh in the audience. He owned the Cafe Gala, and Eadie and Rack played superb piano there. Then Phil Shelley called to say that Walsh was selling his club and the new owner wanted me to audition on Sunday night.

The Cafe Gala had once been a private house, a substantial home off Sunset Boulevard in that area just between the Los Angeles city limits and the edge of Beverly Hills. It had latterly become a radiant jewel of a nightclub. Downstairs was a dining room and a salon—one long continuous sweep with French doors leading out to a garden. Beyond a wall with a huge window set in its center was the bar and through the window a view of the city, that twinkling, bugle-beaded sight called Los Angeles. Everything in the main room was red and white, the striped walls, the banquettes, and the tablecloths. Even the matchbooks were red, with a Venetian mask evocative of carnival time, fiesta, revelry— and the waiters wore white gloves.

Two people had opened the place a few years before, one with an imposing name, particularly for the West Coast in 1942: Catherine, the Baroness d'Erlanger, born Marie Rose Antoinette de Robert d'Agueria de Rochegude, had married into the distinguished European banking family of d'Erlanger. Even the greenest and most unsophisticated kid in Los Angeles would realize that was a mighty impressive name on a first-class European family tree. In Europe she was a patroness of the arts with an entourage of serious composers, authors, and painters as well as a circle of cabaret and music hall performers. With her husband, Baron Emile Beaumont d'Erlanger, she had owned a town house in London, where her salon rivaled those in Paris ruled by Louise Vilmorin and American heiress Winaretta Singer, who became the Princesse de Polignac. There Catherine had discovered a group called the Australian Boys and become sponsor and mentor to one of them, a handsome and clever fellow named John Walsh. Widowed before the outbreak of war and fearing the threat of fascism, Catherine came with her protégé to America.

I saw her often seated on one of the red corner banquettes, spouting orders in French to an expatriate waiter. Did they know in Hollywood that this larger-than-life woman with fiery red hair had been painted by Romaine Brooks and had arranged Diaghilev's funeral in Venice? Gossips said that her title was real—and that her emeralds were supposed to be glass. They sure looked real to me.

With the superb support of John Walsh, she opened the Cafe Gala. It didn't take long for it to become the last word in supper clubs out west—as *they* said, "on the Coast." Any traveler leaving Los Angeles boasted of having been there—even if he was lying. It was *the* place to be.

John Walsh was no neophyte; with years of international experience in musicals and cabarets, he was a real pro. He placed two grand pianos below the arches at the garden end of the cafe, knowing the place was small enough not to need a sound system. Backed by the masterful accompaniment of Eadie and Rack he treated his discriminating clientele to an endless repertoire of carefully chosen songs, to special music, to the special sound of that special world—the precious and protected smart supper club.

There he held sway with gems like "September Song," often throwing in a zany waltz celebrating love called "It's a Big, Wide,

Wonderful World," written by John Rox and most identified with Nancy Nolan, who sang it nightly at New York's Monkey Bar in her inimitable whiskey voice.

At the Gala—and everyplace performers could be seen and heard—I was all eyes and ears, picking up on any new melody, tracking it down, and sizing it up for my own possible use. Some material didn't seem to mesh with my style and abilities. Many Noel Coward songs seemed above my reach; later I realized that nobody sang Coward better than the master himself. If the words of Cole Porter's "I'm a Gigolo" seemed too arch, too sophisticated, I tried to figure out how to make the song fit the image I projected. My youth was working against me, and I leaned toward songs with a lighter comedy edge and idyllic love songs like "My Romance" that worked particularly well—yet I was drawn to more grown-up lyrics. Oh, how superior and intellectual I felt when I sang them, as if I'd been reading Aldous Huxley. Words were poetry to me, even before I knew who had written the lyrics. I never knew who Vernon Duke was the day in Omaha when I bought Hildegarde's record album of his work, I was simply drawn to the songs. And after a few years I had collected enough obscure material and enough know-how to hold my own with anyone willing to discuss such things. To this day I can hear a Broadway score with three hits in it and find a fourth number that suits me better. The best advice came from Phil Moore, who put it very plainly one afternoon: "Robin, what you want to do is perfect an act that you can take *anywhere* and perform for *anybody*. When you start learning new songs, keep that in mind."

Into the Gala came exiled royalty, movie stars, and studio moguls—New Yorkers stuck in Hollywood for a picture made the club their headquarters. Cole Porter and Monty Woolley spent their evenings there—everybody said it was fun, more fun than any other place between the Pacific and the East Side of Manhattan.

Leo James Dolan was from San Francisco, where he owned a successful bar bearing his name. In 1948 he thought he was getting John Walsh and Eadie and Rack when he bought the Gala. Instead he heeded Walsh's advice when told that he would do just fine with a fellow named Bobby Short and a young comedienne appearing in a new intimate revue in Hollywood. On a Sunday night I went in to play for James Dolan and was hired on the spot. Unfortunately he was not enchanted by the tall, blond lady of the revue. Months later he was alone and out of step,

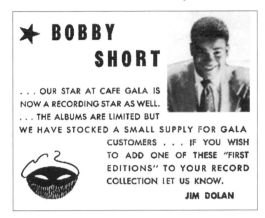

★ **BOBBY SHORT**

. . . OUR STAR AT CAFE GALA IS NOW A RECORDING STAR AS WELL. . . . THE ALBUMS ARE LIMITED BUT WE HAVE STOCKED A SMALL SUPPLY FOR GALA CUSTOMERS . . . IF YOU WISH TO ADD ONE OF THESE "FIRST EDITIONS" TO YOUR RECORD COLLECTION LET US KNOW.

JIM DOLAN

but without regret, when New York went mad for her in the same show: *Lend an Ear*. It was Carol Channing's Broadway debut.

Trying to fill Johnny Walsh's shoes was a rather herculean task for James Dolan. Those shoes, like everything else John wore, were custom made. Classically handsome, a distinguished figure in front of the two pianos—with impeccable manners and easy style—he was the gracious host, singing a song or welcoming a new act. It was no simple task to attempt to step into those hand-stitched shoes. But Dolan was a gambler through and through—he was willing to chance it.

And he knew the key word was "elegance."

We had a packed house on opening night. Marilyn Williams was the singer. Fresh from London with her accompanist. Her mother, Marion Harris, had been popular in speakeasy days before moving to England. Marilyn had style, and she knew many people to help fill the room. My pals didn't let me down, either. Among them was agent Al Kingston, a loyal follower since Trocadero days. After the first show he had a suggestion: "How about leading off with an instrumental medley, Bobby? After all, they just heard the girl singing. Do something brilliant at the piano before your first song." I tried it for my second show, and it worked.

I soon realized that Marilyn was using the Gala to gain some attention and to move out quickly—onto a broader American scene. Phil Baker, the veteran musical man and vaudevillian, had been her mother's partner and was about to star in a revue on the road before taking it to New York. She changed her name to Marion Harris Jr., and off she went, to sing "Would You Like to Take a Walk?" and "Blue Again" to Baker's accordion accompaniment.

Dolan had to start auditioning new acts. Fran Gregory was a local product with a good voice and lots of friends. The regular Gala clientele was coming in every night, and the club was small enough to look and feel crowded even at only half capacity. But Dolan was in full command. He played master of ceremonies like Johnny Walsh before him. With his toothy smile he made a brave attempt to mimic the Walsh mannerisms. He found a second pianist as well as Roland Gerbeau, a romantic crooner straight from Paris.

"I want you two to go down to Hollywood Boulevard and get measured for new tuxedos," he told us one evening. "We've got to look swank around here."

Obviously, Jim Dolan didn't approve of my New York clothes, but it was a generous gesture. No boss I knew ever paid for a performer's clothes. McIntosh was a tailor of stature, in business for years, a shop from the old days. Framed shots announced that Warner Baxter and George Brent were clients—and in a week I was wearing the most shaped, padded, and buckramed tuxedo. A suit to pose in, perhaps, surely not meant for easy movement. Sitting at the piano for the first show, I was barely able to breathe, let alone move.

Jim Dolan was so pleased by the way we looked, he had

ordered a McIntosh suit for himself—the same padding, the same nipped-in shape at the waist. He was about Alan Ladd's height, definitely not tall. In his stiff new suit he was miles away from making it à la Johnny Walsh.

I never knew if he noticed how I got into that lining and cut away the padding before performing the next night. Whew, what a relief—I was breathing again!

My contract for two weeks with options had been forgotten. The situation was pleasant, and we went along smoothly. I was satisfied, aside from the salary—a skimpy $150 a week, out of which came ten percent for Phil Shelley. The hours were decent, and we drew a quality crowd. A new neon sign on the roof was flashing on and off in red letters—"Jim Dolan presents Bobby Short." Dolan had hired a press agent. The image was changing. Maybe it was not what Johnny Walsh had stood for. But now it was Dolan's Gala.

Driving around Los Angeles, you saw the signs all over town, announcements of the latest lineup at the club. There were ads in the trades, the daily papers, too. We were only a cut or two below the larger popular establishments like Mocambo and Ciro's. And as our fame grew—that is, Dolan's fame—performers of stature were attracted to the Gala. From New York's Rainbow Room Dolan persuaded Elizabeth Talbot Martin, a talented monologuist, to join the bill. Harry Noble and Frances King added their glowing presence from time to time. He played the piano, and they both sang his irresistible arrangements. Jean Arnold, who went on to become a successful Broadway actress, made her cabaret debut at the Gala.

Oddly enough, Dolan was showing up at the club less and less. True, it seemed to run by itself, but someone else was in evidence now. Preston Young was part of the Dolan entourage from San Francisco, a clever young fellow who learned every nuance of operating the Gala. Attractive in a Brooks Brothers way, Preston knew how to welcome the guests, operate the lights—and in no time at all he made it quite apparent that Jim Dolan's presence was not needed.

However, Dolan's occasional visits were welcome ones, though the cafe was managed well when he was not around. He had kept the devoted crew. The faithful Myrna had come from Belgium years before and stayed to oversee the waitresses who replaced the waiters of Johnny Walsh's heyday. Upstairs were Catherine Auth, handling the books, and Zoia, the cashier, a White Russian who somehow had landed at the Gala after touring with the old *Chauve-Souris* revue.

I knew that Cole Porter was one of the faithful when Johnny Walsh and the Baroness reigned at the Gala, but I had no idea he had been in since my opening . . . until Fran Gregory asked me to play for her at an audition—for the national company of *Kiss Me Kate*. Fran was performing at the club, singing the songs of Bianca, the role that made Lisa Kirk an overnight star on Broadway—and Fran thought this was her big chance. We drove down to the Masonic Temple, and hours later the fulsome applause we heard was from the composer himself. Grinning, Cole Porter leaned forward on his chair next to the producer and director. "Bobby," he asked me, "do you do any of the songs from Kate?"

I was dumbstruck—not only had he been at the Gala, but he had heard me sing. I had been doing "Too Darn Hot" since the show had opened. Now I sang it, and there was more applause.

At the end of the week I was still singing "Too Darn Hot" at the club. The *Kiss Me Kate* part was written for a dancer—and a dancer I definitely was not.

But my name was flashing from the sign on the roof of the Gala, my spot seemed assured, and I had the prestige of being the closing act. Aside from all this eminence, I was the emcee, I accompanied some of the singers, and I often played in-between music when no performer was on. I was all over the place, sometimes checking coats and even reeling off the champagne list to Lady Sylvia Ashley. The learning process was in progress.

More and more New York exiles arrived at the club. The Broadway theater surrendered a sterling group to MGM—Vincente Minnelli and Gene Kelly, Kay Thompson, Betty Comden and Adolph Green, designers Lemuel Ayers and Irene Sharaff. Roger Edens, who had accompanied Ethel Merman when she made her New York bow in *Girl Crazy*, was their ringleader. A tall man with a deep voice, a gravelly Southern accent, and tremendous style and wit, Roger was the major influence on Judy Garland's early pictures—he had written "Dear Mr. Gable" for her. Producer Arthur Freed brought this group together in what became the famous Freed Unit.

When I first saw Lena Horne I suppose I behaved like a million of her other fans. I was much too stunned by her beauty to speak. It was pure delight to see her come through the door with her husband, Lennie Hayton, the ace music arranger at Metro. They had been loyal patrons since the John Walsh days.

Lena relaxed at the Gala. Quite often she and Lennie invited me along with them for a nightcap and something to eat at their place in Nichols Canyon. Not a long drive to their unpretentious house, all of it comfortable and easy, with a beautiful gray cat roaming around the place and sometimes wandering off to the house up the hill to visit a playmate at James and Portland Mason's.

Very often Lena and Lennie stayed on after closing time. He took over at the other piano, and with the two of us playing, Lena would sing. What luck for the late customers, getting this unexpected finale! Sometimes we would go on for hours; Preston would lock the front door, and the bar was kept open.

All Hollywood eventually came to the Gala. What better place for an evening out than our intimate club, where everyone wound down after the pressures of a day at the studio. No formalities, a casual atmosphere and easy attitude on the part of the protective professional staff.

Show folk were not the only customers at the Gala; what was called "real people" came in as well, some from old-line California society enclaves—Pasadena, Santa Barbara, San Marino—many from other parts of the country, particularly the South. I wondered why. Not since St. Louis had I had any close contact with Southerners or been exposed to their feelings and their manners. Well, they came to be entertained like anyone else—they had the money and were looking for a good time. Some nights I thought the little room was going to sink under the weight of Southern accents—"Bobby, why don't y'all come down to Dallas, y'heah? They'll just luv ya at the Bay-kah Hotel!" I'd close my eyes and think that I was in Dixie.

From the roster of visitors came some steady friendships. A young couple arrived from Tulsa—the son of a successful gas-tank manufacturer and his wife who had been the prettiest girl in town. She still was, and nice, too. Jay P. Walker, Jr. and Molly were new regulars at the club after they became residents in nearby Brentwood. I quickly realized that Jay was a voracious reader with an impressive library, and the Walkers' interest in food and good restaurants matched mine. It didn't take long before we were often seeing each other outside the Gala. When they were on hand at the club Molly, chic to the teeth, sat up front, mouthing the lyrics as I sang.

Their house had an enormous pool and a beautiful garden. They drove a 1949 black convertible Cadillac with fishtails and red leather upholstery. For the summer they moved out to a beachfront condominium in Malibu, and I was included in everything they did. I had bought my first car back in 1947 and found myself scooting around town to meet them for dinner or lunch downtown before a matinee.

And I met B. J. Adler—"B.J." was something that I guessed she had trumped up rather than enduring Betty Jean or Barbara Jean. She came from an extraordinary background. Her paternal grandmother had been a Rosenwald, from the philanthropic Chicago family. The Rosenwald Apartments was a legendary housing complex for Negroes as far back as I could remember. B.J. lived with her father and two younger sisters in an imposing house in Beverly Hills, and other members of the family lived nearby. On Monday evenings I was invited to her house for dinner, and on Fridays her grandmother took us to the afternoon symphony concerts. We went with the Walkers to the ballet and the opera, sometimes for a meal at a Santa Monica restaurant of the moment.

After we had been seen around town together for a while, an item appeared in a local gossip column saying that we were to be married—the Gala press agent obviously was working overtime, perhaps inspired by the recent marriage of black singer Billy Daniels to a white East Coast socialite. But B.J. remained her cool, serene self, and we went on having our Monday night dinners, going to our symphony matinees and making a round of parties on my nights off.

On weekends after my last show, a group of us would go for a nightcap to Leonard Spiegelgass's house only a few blocks away. A big-time screenwriter with a piercing wit and sharp tongue, he held court at these midnight soirees surrounded by his expensive furniture, his paintings, and a collection of esoteric records, expounding on everything from the Broadway theater to the latest literary rage in Paris—or politics, taking special pleasure in finding an unsuspecting victim upon whom he could level his seemingly vast awareness and knowledge. After going on about injustice in the movie industry, as Fritzi Masarry songs from Noel Coward's *Operette* played on his record player, he steered the conversation to one of his favorite subjects—the inequity between American whites and Negroes. Suddenly he was leaning toward B.J., his finger waggling. "And what have *you* done to help solve this dilemma in our society?"

B.J. didn't waste a second. In her composed manner, fluttering her long lashes, she answered in the sweetest voice, "All I know is that my grandfather gave the Negroes fifty million dollars so I could go out with Mr. Short." There was a round of applause from everyone in the room.

Dinner invitations came often now, at houses that were more than grand—after all, it was Beverly Hills. I was becoming a fixture on the Hollywood scene. I sure didn't like facing that my career was in a rut. But at the same time it seemed that there was no limit to my social progress. Lee and Ira Gershwin had asked me to perform for them at their Beverly Hills home. I was even, to quote Lorenz Hart, invited to several parties "where they honored Noel Ca'ad."

The list of entertainers at the Gala changed more quickly than the seasons. Pianists seemed to come and go, lady singers were in and out. But once in a while an act appeared with a magic touch. One of those rarities was Bobby Troup. When Jim Dolan persuaded Bobby to bring in his trio, a new ingredient was added to the Gala menu and a new audience as well. Bobby's "Route 66" and "Daddy" were tremendously popular, a more middle-of-the-road trend that proved successful.

Another was Stella Brooks. Stella was hip beyond her years and her time, touted in *The New Yorker* as a great jazz singer. But she was more than that. Her wit was rapierlike, and her following included such diverse types as Lucius Beebe and Marlon Brando. She had little patience with inattentive or unsophisticated audiences, and she did not suffer fools. One evening at a party where she had performed, one of the guests approached her when she was finished. He asked whether she was colored or white. Losing not a beat, she shot out that whatever color she happened to be was her own business. The next question was how much it would cost to have her sing at a party he was planning. Stella, ever ready with a comeback, informed him that it depended—did he want to hire her as a colored singer or a white one? As you might imagine, I loved this Stella story.

Jerry Reilly, the publicist, managed to get *Variety* and the *Hollywood Reporter* to review our shows. Now the mainstay of the bill, I was getting more than my share of good notices—and sometimes constructive criticism when David Hanna of the *Reporter* or Mike Kaplan of *Variety* reviewed us. I had added Bessie Smith's old classic "Gimme a Pigfoot" to the repertoire, and though the crowd loved it, Kaplan disagreed, printing that, in his view "Bobby Short can follow anything on the current bill with ease. But he can't follow Bessie Smith."

I had learned that many things I admired were not for me when I tried them out with the audience. Risqué material simply didn't suit me. Was I too young? Did my wide eyes negate such worldly suggestions?

Molly and Jay Walker took off from California at the same time every year to visit their parents in Tulsa. Before leaving, they always presented me with a stash of goodies from their larder. It was like Christmas—cases of imported beer, wonderful wine, all kinds of delicacies. Jay called early one morning, talking quickly in his usual breathless way.

"Bobby, Molly and I are talking about selling the car," he was saying. "We think you should buy it. You can't keep driving around town in that beat-up old coupé of yours. You're a star on the Sunset Strip and you ought to own a nice car."

I explained that the financial obligations I was living under prevented any new expenses. When I told him the payment on my old Dodge was $85 a month, he suggested that I take on the Cadillac and pay $75 a month against whatever the list price was on the used-car market. When the Walkers left for Oklahoma the following week, I drove them to the airport and rode home in my new car.

With the convertible top down, I drove around town the way the Walkers wanted me to, and I loved every minute of it. Downtown to the theater on my night off, inviting friends along to an after-hours bar when I finished at the club—or to the drugstore at the Beverly-Wilshire. There, in the coffee shop that stayed open all night, we could order a snack or a full Chinese dinner. If the hostess didn't have a table, we could scan shelves of everything from $1,000 brush sets to bottles of aspirin and cure-alls. Sometimes we'd stop at Hamburger Hamlet, which had been opened by two enterprising actors, Marilyn and Harry Lewis, where we were served by waiters biding their time until the big movie break came along. Having a late bite to eat was absolutely the Hollywood thing to do.

Often Rose Davies, sister of the famous Marion who lived at San Simeon, dropped by the Gala on her way home from the races. In simple day clothes, but covered with diamonds, she stayed for both shows and then insisted on bringing a crowd up to her house in Bel-Air for drinks and food. No matter how late it was, her butler was ready to serve, and walking through the entryway, I always saw the same load of luggage—I wondered if it was baggage that had not been unpacked or if it just sat there in case she wanted to make a quick getaway.

Business at the club was great, though my salary was not keeping pace. Suddenly the customers were the ones surprising and entertaining the performers, quite a reversal in pattern. And the antics of some patrons were pretty riveting. One faithful customer would spend the evening drinking steadily, then rise from his chair with great caution and move toward the bar in a stiff but even walk, to be met by a pair of attendants ready to usher him into an ambulance waiting out on the street.

One night a woman arrived in a wheelchair, and when she reached a front table stepped nimbly from the chair to her favorite banquette—where she sat until the show was over and the chair was wheeled back to roll her out of the club.

Betty Rowland, once a reigning burlesque queen, caught the late show one night and was completely carried away by one of my songs. She applauded loudly and followed me out to the bar, whooping all the way. "Baby, if I could dance while you played and sang, we'd have some act!" She threw her arms around me and leaped into the air, fastening her legs around my waist; then, as she released her hold on my neck, she fell backward, her hair dragging on the floor. She hung on to me as I carried her to the front door.

Ronnie Quillan had quite a reputation as a girl about town. She always came into the Gala wearing one of what was rumored to be a closetful of mink coats over a Joan Crawford–inspired evening gown. With her red hair glowing, she had the look of a glamorous relic, a stunning presence from some other time. One night during a set I spotted Ronnie in the bar—in a furious fist-fight with another woman. I went on with my song, though it was like watching a Punch and Judy show. I finished the song, and then the audience's attention was drawn to the ruckus behind them. Now all eyes were on the battle out in the bar, until Dolan rushed into the fray. Ronnie was asked to leave—never to return. Then three weeks later she reappeared, another mink coat, another Crawford-like gown—and when she saw Jim Dolan she handed him a gold Cartier cigarette case. In it was three thousand dollars—all of it his if she ever behaved badly again. He accepted, of course, and stepped aside to allow her passage into his enchanted cottage.

We were laughing and having a good time, never knowing what new and peculiar capers were in store for us. But, despite the success I was having, Jim Dolan never thought of raising my salary. I had a new apartment for $75 a month, the same amount as my car payment. Phil Shelley was getting his usual ten percent. I was sending money to my mother back in Danville. All that and keeping my wardrobe up to snuff left little spare change. Repeatedly, I asked Jim for more money, and repeatedly, he turned me down. I was sure it would not be easy to replace me, but I knew Jim Dolan—he would try.

He found Robert Clary, a young French singer playing at another club. A natural performer with faultless timing and an appealing personality, Clary drew a crowd of devotees.

From New York and the Blue Angel, Jim Dolan was bringing in a singer the *Saturday Review* critic said had a voice from the gods: Portia Nelson. It was Betty Mae, my old buddy from the Alvino Rey days in Chicago, newly first-named for the stoic soap-opera heroine of *Portia Faces Life*. The critic had not exaggerated. Portia walked onto the floor of the Gala, tall, poised, goddesslike in floating chiffon—and singing in a way that was all her own. She was a smash.

Politics was in the air around us every day and in the nightly doings at the cafe as well. The sad saga of the Hollywood Ten was on: the McCarthy inquisition played itself out on television and in the papers. To say that anything construed as "Red" made everyone nervous was an understatement.

I have never mixed preaching and entertaining. Clearly, I was no Leadbelly, and songs heavily laden with messages about the rights of man are not for me. But songs come along that allow me to speak my mind without getting on a soapbox. Rodgers &

Hammerstein had written such a song for *South Pacific*. The lyrics of "Carefully Taught" made it clear that racial prejudice is instilled in people in as structured and careful a way as any of the other things they learn early in life. *South Pacific* was an enormous hit in New York, and I had been singing "Carefully Taught" along with "Bali Ha'i" and "Honey Bun" as a salute to the show. The number never failed to bring cheers from the audience. And I hoped it made them think.

Another Richard Rodgers song from the thirties had pointed lyrics by Lorenz Hart. "Too Good for the Average Man" listed the luxuries of the rich, satirically showing what disaster they led to. One night I had just gone into the verse with "When Russia was white, it was white for the classes and black for the masses" when a Hollywood leading man known for his right-wing politics reacted with "Oh, for Christ's sake!" and, with his ladyfriend right behind him, went stomping out of the room.

A couple of years before, New York had had another musical with a sensational score. *Finian's Rainbow* was by Burton Lane and E. Y. Harburg, with a loud and distinct message that sometimes seemed ridiculous. The feelings expressed so openly were a major surprise at a time when many people were suspicious of even their best friends being so-called fellow travelers. The ideas in the songs were simple truths that could offend no one—if they were really listening.

And as my finale I often sang one of them, "When the Idle Poor Become the Idle Rich," with Yip Harburg's great phrases and fanciful double entendre:

> And when all your neighbors are upper-class,
> You won't know your Joneses from your Ass-tors.
> When we all have ermine and plastic teeth,
> How will we determine who's who underneath?

The crowd loved it. I finished the song one night and walked round the piano for a deep bow, and as I raised my head I realized that a man was standing right in front of me. He was in his sixties, wearing a white linen suit that matched his snowy hair and mustache—and talking to me during the ongoing applause. As I tried for a graceful exit, I could tell that his words were all sorghum and corn bread.

"Why do you sing that terrible Communist song?" I was in a scene foolish enough to be in *Finian's Rainbow*, and now the Colonel was following me into the hall. "Boy, why are you singing this awful music? Don't you know something patriotic and American to do for the folks?" He would not stop. "Something like 'My Old Kentucky Home' or some spirituals. . . ."

"Or 'Old Black Joe'?" I threw in. This suggestion obviously seemed to please him. Suddenly there was Portia Nelson at my side, looking glorious in her Charles James, apparently sensing trouble and ready for it.

Her arm went around my shoulder, her voice sugar sweet as she asked, "What's the matter, darling, everything all right?"

Now our nonplussed Colonel was really raving on. "Why, my God, this whole place is a hotbed of Communists!" With this sputtered conclusion, he was off in a cloud of his own cigar smoke.

On balance we were a pretty impressive group at the Gala. Portia and Robert Clary, Bobby Troup, and me: a roster that generally worked for the audience. And I wondered how much Jim Dolan appreciated us.

The man had always been ambitious, and now he was looking for ways to expand his operations. Sometimes his methods seemed something short of honorable. For a time he disappeared with the weekend receipts just before payday, not a habit anybody at the club appreciated. And after five or six episodes I announced that I would not come into work on Monday unless he paid me in cash for the previous week. Dolan brought this on himself; cash was necessary after too many bouncing checks. His movements were always a mystery, and his bad checks aggravated my disrespect, magnifying his refusal to raise my salary. Suddenly he suggested that I take a few weeks off.

This was a new low for him. Across the street a new place had opened—it was called the Blue Angel, not the most original name for a club. There were turnaway crowds every night for an act called Tony and Eddie—two fellows who mimed to records. I had seen them a few times—they were hilarious, acting out wild shenanigans to very familiar songs by very familiar singers. Dolan saw a future with them and thought it a good idea to be rid of me for a while.

Enough was enough. I had stayed in Jim Dolan's enchanted cottage too long—it was time to look for another job. There were choices. Along La Cienega and on the Strip quite a few new spots had opened. However, there was also the Haig—John Bennett came up with an offer. And there I could be king of the hill. To avoid any doublespeak from Dolan, saying I had not given him adequate notice, I went to the musicians union. Their advice was to send him a telegram—with copies to them—to prove that I was giving him proper notice, should he try to keep me from working anywhere else.

Ego told me they'd miss me on the Strip, but with Bennett I'd be more comfortable—and he had offered me a hefty pay hike.

For the next few months old friends from the Gala were lining up at the Haig to see me. The Walkers came in night after night, B.J. brought her group—and thanks to Jerry Reilly, a new crowd was finding the way to John Bennett's saloon. Reilly consented to do press for me at a reasonable fee, and he was doing good work. I was off in the right direction—again.

Over at the Gala, Jim brought in Fifi D'Orsay. She was the movie star from Canada who in the thirties had charmed her audiences with a *ver-ee* French accent—and had never been to France. Then he booked the Bando da Lua, the quartet who backed Carmen Miranda in her movie musicals. It was Dolan's lucky day when Phil Moore arrived in town and decided that the Gala was *the* perfect place to present Dorothy Dandridge. Moore was the expert arranger, coach, and manager who had worked with Lena Horne years earlier. Dorothy had been around for some time, performing without any definition or direction. Now, after months of studying and listening to Phil, she was ready. And the whole town was talking—she was an instant sensation. I could not help a feeling of pride that Jerry Reilly had a hand in Dorothy's success with his publicity sleight of hand.

I could have stayed on Wilshire Boulevard for a year with the crowds that kept coming in week after week. A man named Neshui Ertegun stopped by one night—I knew his name because of his reputation as the Jazz Man. He had a great collection of hard-to-get music at his shop on La Cienega. His brother was with him—Ahmet, head of Atlantic Records in New York and responsible for putting the work of Mabel Mercer, Cy Walter, and many terrific rhythm and blues performers on his label. The tall, distinguished fellow with them was introduced to me. "This is Vernon Duke. . . ." I couldn't believe it—one of my all-time idols, in the Haig to hear what I was going to play. It didn't take long for him to join me at the piano, accompanying me on "April in Paris" and "What Is There to Say?"

I had mixed emotions when I heard that business at the Gala slipped after Dorothy Dandridge's engagement was over. Jerry Reilly was always first with the latest news—it was no surprise then to pick up the phone and hear him say that Jim Dolan wanted me to return to the Gala. He was willing to pay me more money, and he guaranteed I would have it on time. Talk about ambivalent feelings! Yet I knew I had to accept Dolan's offer. I

JIM DOLAN *presents*
at
Cafe gala

THE SONGS AND
INIMITABLE PIANO STYLINGS
OF
BOBBY SHORT
Commencing . . .
WEDNESDAY
AUGUST 8th
1 9 5 1
With . . .
8 7 9 5   S U N S E T   B O U L E V A R D

insisted on giving John Bennett an extended notice. Then I was back at the Gala.

Business was good from the start, with familiar faces in the audience—Lena and Lennie, Pearl Bailey, Roger Edens, Barbara and Margaret Whiting. The Beverly Hills movie group, the society crowd, and the usual visiting firemen from the East. New faces, too—Gracie Allen and George Burns, Ella Logan. And Jerome Kern's widow, Eva, with the great singer George Byron, who would become her next husband. One evening, Rita Stone, one of my most devoted fans, dropped by on the arm of Johnny Stompanato.

But the most satisfying new face to see at the Gala was Mrs. Short. My mother, at last, came to visit—and at the sight of her in the audience I was for a sudden moment back in Danville, little Bobby Short playing to make Mother proud. That same night,

Bobby Troup's mother was sitting across the room. Mrs. Troup came over to Mother's table, and in a second they were deep in conversation—I had no idea what they were discussing so intently, but obviously they found a lot to talk about. I wondered—was it "mother talk"? And was Mrs. Short remembering the old upright and her boy Bobby picking out "Who?" back in Danville such a long time ago?

In spite of the happy moments, in spite of my new salary, a Brooks Brothers charge account, and spare cash for repairs on the Cadillac, I kept asking myself if shuttling back and forth from the Haig to the Gala was really taking my career anywhere. I was hearing the same promises, going to the same parties. I never considered myself transparent, but one evening Jay and Molly Walker talked to me. They sensed the way I felt—what's more, they agreed with me when we talked about my apathy and this rut I was in.

"Bobby, why don't you go to Paris?" Jay asked.

Paris had always sat in the back of my mind. It was Mecca, especially if you were black and wanted to get ahead. But the question was always how, and that was what I asked Jay now. "How, how?"

"Hell, Bobby," he said, "you can sell the damned car, can't you!"

A maiden trip . . . an aeroplane . . . "
Singing them here tonight at the Carlyle, Cole Porter's
words bring back memories. "Pilot Me" was written in
the late twenties, and I sing it because its double entendre always tickles the audience. As I do the lyrics in
French and then in English, I remember those last few
weeks after I listened to Jay Walker's advice to sell the
car and fly away to France. "An aeroplane . . . a cozy,
narrow plane . . ."

I can still hear the questions they were asking—the
specific voices may be gone, but not the tone of disbelief.
Where will you go in Paris, who are your friends there?
Who is your agent, where will you work? And, really,
how important is Paris? The same questions over and
over again. What skeptics! And I wondered if it was
because they were too afraid to move their own butts.

Looking back now, I realize how swiftly fate stepped
in, that conjurer's hand from out of nowhere—and
within the space of only a couple of weeks. From out of
the blue a magician appeared—an agent—and all the
wrinkles were ironed out, without risk, without any real
moves from me—and I *was* going to Paris.

David Stein was more than a magician who walked

into the Gala before I closed there—he was the brother of Jules Stein who owned Music Corporation of America, the great talent agency with offices in Paris as well as Hollywood and New York and London. David headed the Paris office, he understood me from the first minute we talked, and he was on his way back to France after visiting his family in Los Angeles. He asked if I knew Bricktop—who hadn't heard of the legendary Brick? The woman who opened her club in Paris in the twenties, who epitomized the glittering world of Scott Fitzgerald and Zelda, who was a character in an Evelyn Waugh novel. Stein thought she would surely have constructive ideas. He would talk to her and look around when he was in Paris—he'd be writing to me.

Only a few weeks later a letter arrived, and I knew what euphoria was. It didn't even matter what he said— he had kept his promise to write. I was astonished. The piece of paper in my hand was a small miracle, and then I saw dates—names—places. David Stein said he knew of a *boîte de nuit*—I knew the word; I hadn't been studying French for nothing. A small nightspot called the Mars Club, owned by an American. Who had heard of me. The letter said I could open at any time I was available. And MCA was going to guarantee engagements for me in London—and Alexandria!

I made my travel reservations, and a passport was next. My mother sent my birth certificate. I thought everything was in order—then one unforeseen problem. When I looked at the certificate I saw that I was listed as "white." She had crossed out the word and in her careful hand had written above it "colored." Had the doctor who delivered me been color-blind? Had Mother never looked at the piece of paper before? I doubted that the State Department was going to honor her personal correction, so the document went back to Danville. Another few weeks and a new certificate arrived. The correction was made, but my date of birth was listed as September 5, not 15. No time for a change—to this day, in the eyes of immigration officials, I am ten days older.

Jerry Reilly came up with an offer for me to work my last two weeks at another spot, the Bar of Music. Mme. Villaudy, the owner's wife, had been scouting me to come over to the large club that was almost a block long and drew an equally large audience. I can see her now—with her Van Dongen eyes and raven hair, chain-smoking and talking in a deep Russian accent. Seeing her for the first time, I thought of Elinor Glyn's *Three Weeks*—and I imagined her being the proprietress of some smoky Montmartre cabaret. Paris was definitely on my mind.

Elsa Lanchester was going to double at the Bar of Music after her revue spot at the Turnabout Theatre, and I would be second on her bill. The money was good, and I needed it for my first-class ticket.

Valaida Snow was performing at the Club Alabam down in the old black section on Central Avenue. She had been an idol of mine for years; I knew that she had starred in European cabaret, made records and movies before the war came and been interned in a concentration camp. Home again, she was dazzling American audiences with her singing and her hot trumpet playing. I thought this another fateful sign—to see her just before I left for Europe. And, when I told her my plans, she smiled and said, "You'll never come back."

Paris
1952

had heard that Josephine Baker was a very superstitious woman. She claimed it was a good sign to arrive in a strange town in the rain. Maybe my landing in Paris was a mixed blessing. It was raining, then the sun came out, and then it showered again. On and off, all afternoon. This was not what I expected. It seemed more like a tropical weather pattern than my image of "Paris in the spring." I walked for miles, looking for a hotel room. Every place was booked. I had thought of everything before leaving home—everything except to make a hotel reservation.

At last, there was a room at the Hotel des Capucines, between the Place Vendôme and the Opéra. A comfortable one with a huge bathroom.

After dinner I headed for the Champs-Elysées to look for the Mars Club. David Stein had said most anyone could point it out. Anyone in the *arrondissement*—in the area, the neighborhood. I was smiling. Laughing. I had just left my hotel room and gone downstairs—in the *ascenseur*—the highly polished brass elevator that led to the lobby. I passed the wood-framed vitrines, the nineteenth-century furniture, all of it *vieux style*—antique, old style. These words, these wonderful French words. Even the name of the hotel and the street—des Capucines—Franciscan nuns. But I hadn't seen any romantic-looking sisters, not a convent in sight. Well, of course I was alert. I was in Paris—France!

I found the Champs-Elysées and knew that this was a moment to stay in my mind forever. All the familiar paintings and photographs I'd seen while I was growing up didn't keep me from feeling thrilled as I stood there. Here it was—*the* Parisian avenue lined with trees, smart shops everywhere, heavy traffic—and tooting horns. I was sure I heard Gershwin's *American in Paris* as I kept on walking.

Preceding page: Me and my chinos. This picture surfaced in a Gap ad in 1994.

I looked at all the bars along the side streets and finally got directions from a friendly bartender who spoke just enough English to get me to the Mars Club. A few streets farther on and I spotted it at the end of an alley called Robert-Etienne, off the rue Marbeuf. I stopped, and all at once the fatigue of the last day, the long flight across the Atlantic, hit me like the wallop of a sledgehammer. I could not take another step. Meeting the boss, seeing the room, would have to wait until I had a good night's sleep.

Coming down Robert-Etienne the next day, I spotted a rather round, cheerful-looking fellow putting the last tacks into a picture on a sandwich board in front of the club. Walking closer, I saw he was installing photographs of me. He turned, instant recognition—and his arms spread wide to welcome me with a bear hug. "Bobby Short—we were expecting you yesterday! When did you get here, where are you staying?"

Ben Benjamin was from Brooklyn. Stationed in France during the war, he had fallen in love with Paris and had come back to be a saloon owner. Another one of the guys who wanted to hear his favorite kind of music while he worked. We stood outside the club, talking in the balmy spring air, before he led me inside.

As he closed the door I noticed all the names scrawled on it, some rather obscure and many more quite well known. A stellar list—Quentin Foster, Muriel Gaines, Honey Johnson, Aaron Bridges, Eartha Kitt, Art Simmons—and I wondered if I'd be asked to add my signature when the engagement was over. The Mars was tiny, very tiny. And the planet theme was obvious in the sparse decor. Cutout pictures, drawings of the astrological signs, placed along the polished walnut walls. Nothing more except for a plethora of cigarettes stuck to the ceiling like stalactites. I thought that many of Ben's customers must be very dexterous smokers. A few steps down from a tin bar was the smallest baby grand I'd ever seen. Lots of tiny round tables surrounded by backless stools and at the rear a checkroom, an alcove that I guessed was the kitchen. And one toilet—I remembered where I was; this was France, the john was used by both men and women.

"Well now, how do you like it?" Ben asked. I saw there was no microphone, but my long run at the Gala had taught me how to project. "A lot of your pals are in town, and they should all be in tonight," Ben said. "The way they've been coming by to ask when you were opening, the place should be packed."

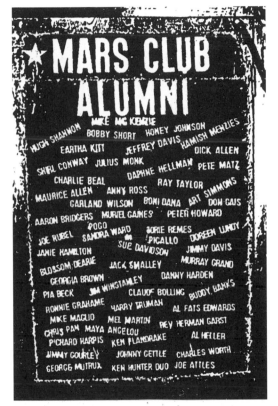

He had made arrangements for me to stay at a nearby hotel; other performers stayed there, and he was sure I'd like it. We walked outside again. This was all so natural, yet it was dreamlike. A place to stay within walking distance, a taxi stand around the corner, shops of every sort close by—and just off the Champs-Elysées!

Ben walked me to a cab. "Don't forget you start your first set at nine," he was saying as the cab pulled away.

"How do I dress?" I called out.

"Any old suit and tie will do," he answered. "We ain't formal here."

Back at des Capucines I laid out a dark blue suit from Brooks Brothers, had my last dip in the Montez pool, and then found another cab. Now I knew it wasn't easy to drive into the *cul-de-sac*—I had another new word—the alley called Robert-Etienne. I walked from the corner to see customers already crowding round the front door.

Smiling faces, many of them familiar. The Mars Club was going to be jammed. It seemed I had only said good-bye to Ella Logan a few weeks ago at the Gala, and here she was. And Arthur Laurents, the playwright, and Richard Hoyt, another regular from Los Angeles. I recognized a face I hadn't seen since I'd worked as a kid in Covington, Kentucky. Here, with his partner Ron Fletcher, was Donn Arden. He was called dance director back then at the Lookout House; now he was the choreographer at the Lido, the famous cabaret on the Champs-Elysées. And Enid Mosier, my old buddy from home, was singing in Paris, too. Mattie, Ann, and Virginia Peters. I had worked with the buxom Peters Sisters in Joliet when Bookie had me on a bill starring Olsen and Johnson. After success at home they had become big stars all over Europe. Ben Benjamin was right—the news of my opening had spread fast.

Before the first set Ben introduced me to his wife. Etla was short, with nothing distinctive about her, nothing I thought was particularly Parisian, though she had an agreeable look. I could not help noticing how she held her position—her own place—at a table close to the front door. In her lap sat a small white dog—the same poodle women in all big cities seemed to love. Fluffy. A surprising name for a dog whose owner spoke no English. I gathered from Ben this was a sore spot—Etla stuck strictly to her native tongue. Floo-fee, she called the little poodle, and boy, was he spoiled. When I met Etla I tried to speak my best French; I had been trying from the minute I'd arrived in Paris the day before. She seemed charmed that I made the effort. Ben's main business was with Americans—American drinks, American food—hamburgers and chili were the special offerings from his minuscule kitchen. Etla made no attempt to mix with her husband's Ameri-

An ad from the Paris Herald Tribune in 1952.

can clientele. However, at the end of the evening I could see how thrilled she was by the crowd and my reception.

Ben wanted to make sure that every American visiting Paris knew about the Mars and his latest attraction. Every day he was at the American Express building, handing out flyers. Not a bad idea. His personal advertising paid off. They were lining up every night at the club. A group that had been on my Air France plane was delighted to have been on the same flight with me. A reporter from the *Daily Mail* in London came in, and he wrote about the Mars a week later. Ben induced Art Buchwald of the *Paris Herald Tribune* to stop by, and a few days later his enthusiastic review appeared in the paper with a photograph. That didn't hurt at all—coming to see Bobby Short at the Mars became the de rigueur thing to do.

It had been thirty years since Josephine Baker took Paris by storm, and the lure was still going on. For an American, the city presented another chance to succeed, to be discovered in a foreign country. For a black entertainer, Paris was a symbol of hope. The race problem was minimal, and performers were judged—glory be—on performance. Paris had offered shelter and much more to black artists—composers, writers, and painters. Richard Wright, James Baldwin, Jacob Lawrence.

A few young composers were at classes with Nadia Boulanger, the great teacher of so many modern giants in the music world, and some of them were customers at the Mars. Thomas Stubbs was one student who came from the Southwest, and though he tried his hand at popular songs, he couldn't coax me to sing one of them. However, he did come up with a far more practical idea. The hotel rate was taking a sizable chunk out of my salary, and Tommy knew a studio was available in his building. He shared an apartment two floors up with a classmate, and he was sure the rent would be a lot more affordable.

The minute I saw the place I knew I had to take it. On the

rez-de-chausée—one more new word! A ground-floor studio—*atelier*, that is. A large room with a huge window covering one wall that faced out to the courtyard. A bath and a kitchen; it was all I needed. I could rent a piano, a Gaveau spinet I had seen. The apartment was on the boulevard de Beau Séjour, which meant "Have a beautiful stay"—the section was called La Muette—the hunting cabin. How could I go wrong? I had a new friend upstairs, and the Benjamins lived just across the road on avenue Foch.

It was May, and Paris was beginning to feel like home. I sent a card on Mother's Day, a greeting from France. How proud my mother would be—something I was sure she had never dreamed of. Hard for me to believe it, too.

Things were humming, and summer came quickly. Every week brought a new throng of tourists. Parisian wine experts were thrilled with the 1952 vintage, the farmers' crops had been abundant, and fashionable visitors were ready to live it up. American-style entertainment was thriving—at the Calvados, the Ringside, and La Fontaine des Quatre Saisons. Spivy's East Side had opened, and the clubs were crowded every night. Up the street from the narrow Robert-Etienne limousines and open sports cars were lining up.

It wasn't long before I learned who was one of my biggest boosters. I had met John Galliher in Hollywood a few years before, and he was living in Paris now. The name *Galliher* meant good looks, charm, and impeccable manners to fashionable hostesses around the world. The classic Yankee, with American-Indian heritage going back to Pocahontas, he divided his time between Paris and London, and if there was something or someone new, John made the discovery first. He lost no time showing up at the Mars every few nights, particularly on Fridays, right after the theater or dinner at Maxim's, in *le smoking*—meaning black tie. The French didn't say "dinner jacket"—and never "tuxedo." Always a crowd with him—the women in bouffant Dior and Jacques Fath dresses that crushed on Ben Benjamin's backless stools. The bartender poured the best champagne rather than the usual *fine à l'eau.* No ordinary brandy and water for John's crowd. Sometimes he had Josette Day with him, the beauty I recognized from the Cocteau movies—and Jean Marais, her leading man—sometimes there was Hubert de Givenchy, who worked with Balenciaga. Etla Benjamin smiled quite a lot on Friday nights.

I knew I was really accepted when invitations kept coming for another Sunday with the Peters Sisters. Any black American hoping to make it in Paris needed approval from the three Peters ladies. They held forth regally in what I imagined was a turn-of-the-century salon on the rue des Belles Feuilles, the "street of Beautiful Leaves"—something out of Proust, only the Proustian menu had been different. Not the scrumptious fried chicken, macaroni with cheese, cauliflower, and beans. Not the deep-dish peach cobbler smothered with whipped cream. The single Proustian touch was the prim and patient serving maid called Françoise.

Nevertheless, I was not taking my good fortune for granted. I had been making 7,500 francs a night, always handed to me in cash by Ben Benjamin, and when the summer business peaked it was raised to 8,500. Not quite $30 in American money—surely not a startling sum, but it matched the salary of a principal at the Lido. Many of the performers who came into the Mars to sip a *fine à l'eau* and see me had to work in two or three places a night to earn something barely comparable. If no work was available, they went off to Brussels or Amsterdam, until another offer came along back in Paris. It seemed as though saloons opened and closed every few minutes: one week a place on the Left Bank, the next one over near the Opéra, all fly-by-night joints taken by some cockeyed optimist hoping to make what the French called *un beau coup*—in American parlance, a killing. The spaces for rent came with tables and chairs, a bar, and sometimes even musical instruments. At the Mars I was safe; business was terrific all summer. In a very short time I had carved out a little niche for myself in Paris nightlife.

Not a bad life, I decided. I had my own apartment—my *atelier*—and with a piano. I began to ask my friends in on Sundays. Enid Mosier came by with bags full of food to prepare in my little kitchen. And could the girl cook! Bud, her husband, was a painter and the name *Mosier*, even though American, was familiar enough for the French to adopt them quickly. A few of the dancers from the Lido came, too. Muriel Gaines was working at the Club de Paris, where she sang everything from Calypso to Trenet to songs of the Auvergne. John Battles had been one of the three sailors in *On the Town*, and had had a major role in *Allegro*. Now he was the lead singer at the Lido and hoping Paris was the city where he would "find himself." With his easy Irish charm and humor he was a clown in the studio, a perfect and beguiling guest. The room buzzed with fast-paced talk, everything and anything from the States and talk about work. Always work—our salaries, our bosses, the French. We talked about their music and how they loved our songs. Enid had tried "My Foolish Heart" in French, John was doing his phonetic best with "St. Louis Blues." Even I had succumbed, putting a few ballads into the act. But finally we all agreed on one thing—we were getting the applause because we were American. And were we all proud of that!

Summer heat hit Paris like a mistral, and the Mars was hot. When I started my first set Ben slammed the front door shut—forty minutes at a high boil. Then with a great flourish he opened the door, and the eager customers fled for air while the new crowd waiting outside filed in.

Air-conditioning was not popular in Paris, despite the heavy

smoke that hung from the low ceilings of most of the saloons, and the Mars was no exception. Ben was not about to take any chances disturbing the residents in the nearby buildings. We all had heard about L'Abbaye over on the Left Bank, where actors Gordon Heath and Lee Peyant worked. The customers leaving and arriving made too merry a sound as the night went on, and local neighbors took to showering them with the contents of their chamber pots. Caution when walking in or out became a habit, and instead of applause an ovation of finger snapping greeted many a performer.

Hugh Shannon and Betty Dodero came in one evening. The two of them made a dash for the piano, Hugh playing "They All Laughed," Betty fanning him as he played, and the two of them singing the Gershwin song. His husky baritone and great piano made him a favorite not only in New York, but in Capri, Southampton, and St. Thomas. Hugh said he preferred working near the sea. This was an act they did together, after Betty divorced the South American millionaire Alberto Dodero.

On another night I spotted a well-dressed couple sitting close to the piano. The waiter told me that a mutual friend of mine had suggested they come in. I went to the table to introduce myself but got no farther than saying my name. The woman stood up. "I'm Dorothy Kilgallen, and this is my husband, Dick Kollmar. Jean Bach asked us to find you." I must have looked puzzled, but she quickly explained that Jean Bach was Jean Cherock—my old friend from Chicago.

I knew the name *Kilgallen*, though her column didn't appear in the L.A. papers. I had never listened to their *Kilgallens* morning radio show, but I had heard Tallulah Bankhead satirize it on her own broadcast. One thing I did know—this was an important lady. I saw an open, winning smile, with her hands moving

Clowning with John Battles.

constantly to accent every word she said. She told me the Bachs were arriving the next day, and asked me if I did "My Funny Valentine."

I watched her out of the corner of my eye as I went through the number. This was one of my favorite Larry Hart lyrics, but it might have been a French art song or a piece of German lieder, she was so completely absorbed, smiling as she led the audience with the loudest applause. I felt I had passed a test.

The following night I had my reunion with Jean Bach—ten years later and here we were in Paris. Light-miles from Chicago, from the Dome at the Sherman. And there was instant rapport the minute I met her husband, Bob. In the next few days I couldn't help noticing how no Parisian gave a damn seeing a pretty blonde hanging on the arm of a black man—unlike the ambience in Chicago a decade before, when I took Helen Canfield Peck to the theater to see *Porgy and Bess*. Tall and striking, Helen was as blond as I was dark. She wore her hair in the Brenda Frazier style of those days, a thick, straight mane. An art student living on Chicago's North Side at the Three Arts Club, she came from conservative horse country in suburban Libertyville, where her mother insisted she jettison her record collection—supposedly to exorcize the demons of jazz, which Helen was crazy about.

The day of our theater date, Helen, after trying a deep leg-makeup tan, with her long blond bob hidden under a turban, finally arrived *au naturel*. We met at our seats, loved the show, and went for coffee to the Oak Room at Walgreen's drugstore—one of the few Loop restaurants where I was welcome. The wildest part of this scenario is that we neither raged nor rebelled. That was just the way it was in the Windy City.

After work at the Mars I took Jean, Bob, and the Kollmars to the Club de Paris for champagne and onion soup. The performers' hangout drew a late-night crowd, and it was no surprise to see Edith Piaf and Anna Magnani in this noisy restaurant where Muriel Gaines sang in the downstairs room. I gave the Bachs and the Kollmars the latest news on the Paris grapevine; in turn, they gave me the scuttlebutt from New York—and with Dorothy Kilgallen at the table, I knew I was hearing it from the horse's mouth. We sipped our wine and played games—word games, song games. "I sing the verse—you sing the chorus!" "I sing a line from a song—you tell me the title!" Then, to make it more difficult, we had to name the composer and guess what show the song came from.

I hated saying good-bye to the Bachs and the Kollmars. Our daily trips around the city, their nightly visits to the Mars were over. The idea that Dorothy might be helpful hadn't entered my mind. I thought about what fun we'd have together if—if I ever got back to New York. Then a week later a letter arrived from Jean—with clippings. Two full columns by Dorothy. In one she wrote about the coming presidential election, the possible new First Ladies, and her recommendations, her pros and cons. "Of course, any First Lady would be a huge success in the White House with Bollinger in the glasses and Bobby Short at the piano." The

Tea with Dorothy Kilgallen at her New York townhouse.

second column told about her trip to Paris, with a rave for my work at the Mars Club.

The phone was ringing early one morning before I poured my coffee. Ben. Asking if I would mind coming by in the afternoon, because he had something to talk to me about. I bathed and shaved, dressed, and went out as I usually did, but Ben's voice was playing over and over in my head. I walked into the empty club and found him working on the soda syphon. He came around to the table near the open door, where the breeze came in from the street.

"Bobby, I want to cut you down to six nights a week," he said the second I sat down.

I immediately thought this was an easy way to lower my salary since David Stein had negotiated a second raise for me, bringing the figure up to 10,000 francs a night. But Ben seemed embarrassed, and I knew him well enough by now to be able to tell. His heart wasn't in this conversation—he didn't like it at all. And I wondered if this had something to do with Etla. For quite a while she had seemed strained with me, not at all the smiling Mme. Benjamin urging me to sing French songs, asking me to lunch once in a while. I'd heard a few bits of gossip from Enid Mosier about the high-handed Etla, and I had to speak up.

"Does this have something to do with your wife?" I asked.

Ben hesitated and then nodded before he went on. Etla wanted him at home more often, and closing one night during the week was going to please her. I had heard about their *mariage de convenance*—being an alien prevented him from owning a business, but as the husband of a Frenchwoman . . . well, that made all the difference, and the authorities were satisfied. Whatever had existed when they were married had now changed. Etla was in love with her immigrant husband.

Well, seven days or six mattered not a whit to me, as long as my salary wasn't slashed. I said this as plainly as possible. The Mars was successful, and it was only the beginning of July.

Ben nodded in agreement, taking my arm when we got up from the bar. "Okay, but, Bobby, when you come in later, try to remember to stop at Etla's table. Talk to her."

Maybe he was right. When I came in I usually went straight to the back for a fast cup of coffee before starting work. Perhaps I didn't pay enough attention to Mme. Mars and Floo-fee.

The legendary Boeuf Sur le Toit reopened, a far cry from the Herbert Jacoby days when Anna Sosenko and Hildegarde had been around. Not at all like the original in the twenties, inspired by Jean Cocteau's famous theater piece with his drawing of a steer on the roof; the renowned hangout of Milhaud and Auric and Poulenc, where Picabia's painting of the evil eye hung on the wall. Now the headliner at the club was June Richmond, a formidable black singer, who had been Jimmy Dorsey's vocalist in America. She had just closed in a revue called *La Tonnerre* and was the rage of Paris. The press was calling her the "Clap of Thunder."

And the Brazilians appeared—I had never seen such an elegant and attractive crowd, all of them rich—they made a great audience with their own samba rhythm, their own sense of timing, and another kind of finger snapping. Years later I was to discover their fierce loyalty. In my New York audiences every night are enthusiastic Paulistos and Cariocas. Then Ethel Smith arrived, the swing organist whose great hit was the song "Brazil." A tiny woman, she wore platform shoes as high as those Carmen Miranda wore in her movie musicals.

Downstairs at the Club de Paris was the *soi-disant*—meaning self-styled—Princess Zena Rachevsky. From Russian royalty on one side of her family and Levi-Strauss on the other, she held forth in the cafe, talking through her repertoire of true Parisian songs in a husky voice while her clientele sipped only champagne Krug.

Liquor manufacturers were popular, giving promotional parties for new products. Lavish parties, where the performers were expected to entertain on the spur of the moment when someone like Schiaparelli turned her salon into a cabaret to push a new brand of Pernod. It was not exactly a joy to sing after too much champagne and a hard night's work—but it was definitely not a dull summer.

One night Lena and Lennie Hayton arrived with Hazel Scott. The well-known jazz pianist had succeeded my good friend Isabelle; she was now Mrs. Adam Clayton Powell. And she drank too much wine, talked too often, and laughed too loud—while I was working. Rudeness from a civilian might not be a surprise, but from another performer!

It was like old home week when the Katherine Dunham dancers came to town. Always a sensation in Europe, they were here in Paris on their annual visit. And did they give new meaning to the Parisian custom of promenade—Vanoye Aikens, Linwood Morris, Frances Taylor (who later became Mrs. Miles Davis), and Julie Robinson, soon to be Mrs. Harry Belafonte. One afternoon I saw Lucille Ellis waving to me from across the street. Her wide smile and obvious joy reminded me of the other brown-skinned American who in the twenties came to Paris and became a legend—Josephine Baker.

Josephine Premice turned up to work at Chez Freddy. I always thought that Jo's innate chic was a result of her French-Haitian background. We didn't see each other often, but when we did it was as if it were yesterday. Yesterday was 1945, when she was on Broadway in a revue called *Blues Holiday*.

The State Department's production of *Four Saints in Three Acts* opened. The Gertrude Stein–Virgil Thompson opera that had caused a stir when it opened in New York years before had an outstanding all-Negro cast. And here were Leontyne Price and Martha Flowers and Betty Allen, with Arthur Mitchell and Louis

Johnson among the dancers. I found them at the Mars, eager to chat, to give me news about life back home.

I met the beautiful Hilda Simms. Like Fredi Washington before her, she was an actress too black to be white and too white to be black—a riddle she was hoping to solve by finding work in France.

All too quickly summer was fading. Now it was Parisians who were showing up at the Mars, along with the few Americans who worked for the government or for private companies. Autumn weather was perfect for strolling the great boulevards, and what a frisson to be greeted as "Monsieur Bobbyshort" the French made my name into one word. And I loved it.

The advent of fall brought a change. Business was winding down, and the Benjamins were complaining. David Stein didn't have any ideas, and in spite of my little fan club, the flurry of excitement was gone like the flower stalls along the streets. I had to start thinking about survival. One solution was to share an apartment with John Battles on the Left Bank. Then I asked Stein to alert his London office about possibilities. He talked about a job in Rio or a room across from the Hotel George V, but nothing happened. The Calvados came along with an offer, but they wanted me to work six-hour stretches. One afternoon, dressed in my best new suit, I had three appointments. At the first office no one was in, at the second the man had just stepped out, and at the third, the person I was to see had simply forgotten.

A few days later I was stopped by a Monsieur Vincent on the Champs-Elysées. He was a backer of Spivy's East Side, and he wanted to know if I would be interested in a club of my own. I went to his office the following day. We spoke about the aspects of planning a club, what kind of salary I would want, how large a room, how long I would stay. And then he floored me. He leaned over his desk and in his most businesslike way asked, *"Monsieur Short, avez-vous une clientele noire assez importante?"* It was his way of finding out whether or not white patrons might object to a sizable black clientele in my club.

I'd heard of this kind of thing happening in the twenties, but I couldn't believe I was hearing it in Paris in 1952. Aside from other Negro entertainers, I knew my Paris audience was definitely white. I could have said so, but I chose not to.

Instead I decided to opt for England. *Bonjour, Londres*!

Hearing the rich, full-bodied laugh, that familiar sound, I know that Marti Stevens is in the room. Sleek and snappy Marti: not only a first-rate actress and singer, but also one of the best mimics alive.

And here I am singing "Tea for Two." What song could be more appropriate for Marti? Marti, my quintessential Anglophile who always starts her day with a "cuppa," who doesn't wake up in the morning bright eyed and bushy tailed, but bright as a marigold.

"Picture you upon my knee . . . me for you and you for me . . ."

I don't remember drinking much tea the first time I was in London, and though I hadn't met Marti then, I do remember quite a lot of running about—I mean running around. In America we go around, in England they go about.

"Tea for two and two for tea . . ."

London

1952

Air France had an early morning flight to London. My appointment was set with a new agent at MCA, and I planned to take a few days to see the city, something I looked forward to. Jock Jacobson was an easygoing, friendly man who welcomed me into his office on Brooke Street, off Piccadilly. I didn't have the goose pimples brought on by the sight of the Champs-Elysées, but it was exciting to walk down the street that was more than familiar from so many lyrics I had been singing for years.

Jock read the press clippings I'd brought along, then called for his secretary, whom I had seen on the plane when I came across the Channel. A good sign, I thought, to be recognized in a flash. "Splendid reviews," he said, looking up from the papers in his hand. "Do you think you'd like to try London for a while? I think we can line up something for you." He reached for the phone, asked for a number, and began talking: "Hello there—Jock Jacobson here. I want to bring somebody over to see you, will you be in for a few minutes? . . . Good, be right there."

Into the street, through a series of arcades and alleyways to Bond Street. "This is the old Embassy Club. Perhaps you can do a couple of tunes for the owners," Jock said, leading me through the side door into a dark vestibule and out to a dance floor lit by one work lamp.

The damask walls were deep red, and the heavy crystal chandeliers gave no reflection in the dim light. The silk-shaded lamps on the white linen table covers were not lit yet, but I could imagine the Prince of Wales with Lady Furness and Mrs. Simpson arriving from the theater in evening clothes—white tie for him and ivory satin bias-cut gowns for the ladies. They were in time for the latest American jazz tunes from the orchestra up on the stage, for

Preceding page: The cover of my first LP for Atlantic Records.

the midnight show. All the glamour of London in the thirties was still vivid here at the Embassy Club.

Jock's voice brought me back to reality, as he introduced the owners of the club. A grand piano was rolled out to the center of the floor. No mike, only the work light, and suddenly an audition was to begin. They applauded after each number, and then we were shaking hands, I was looking at their smiling faces.

"Would you like to come over to the Embassy for a few weeks?" one of the owners asked. The broadest of smiles was on Jock's face.

Money was to be discussed later. He could arrange something quite nice, he claimed. "Have you heard of Bobby Breen?" he wanted to know.

I thought of one of the games I had played only a few months ago with the Kollmars and the Bachs—"Whatever became of . . ."—a name was thrown at you, and someone was supposed to tell what happened to an obscure or long-forgotten star. I knew about Bobby Breen from childhood days on the vaudeville circuit: a boy soprano who had been discovered by Eddie Cantor and gone on to make movies in the Deanna Durbin period. I had done a few of his songs in those days.

"We kept him working here for as long as he wanted to stay," Jock was saying. "We can do the same for you."

I flew back to Paris, and the following week the confirming telegraph came. I was off to London.

A good-looking announcement was mailed to the Embassy clientele—I was going to wear my dinner jacket for the first time in months—dinner and late supper were offered by the management. Two orchestras played for the dancing crowd—the first playing popular songs—most of which I knew from Los Angeles ten years ago. The other band was Cuban—the Latin rhythms currently adored by London night owls. Then, just before midnight, the music stopped, the piano was rolled out, and as the lights dimmed, I was announced. Forty-five minutes later I took a deep bow and a stroll around the ringside tables to express my gratitude for a terrific response. My first show as over.

London was cold and foggy; the evening darkness began right after lunch. But the streets were jammed with shoppers—Christmas was only a few weeks away. London, despite the pain of postwar shortages, was ready for the holidays. Theater was booming, and the shops were crowded with people buying tempting merchandise they hadn't seen for years.

The British tabloids were filled with stories about the black American star at the Colony who was having trouble with her future in-laws. Pearl Bailey was piquing the interest of English readers. She was going to marry a white man—and I was astonished by the badgering she was getting in the daily papers.

When I tracked her down at her hotel, she told me it was true—but never mind, her fellow was coming over. Bellson, just incidentally, was one of the best jazz drummers in the world. And despite his midwest parents' objections, she and Louis were going to be married. I spent a lot of time with Pearl, and one night I managed to shift the time of my show to see her at the Colony.

Pearl literally reached out to her audience when she was performing—and won them over in one huge embrace. Her easy banter, her unpretentious style, were endearing. They always worked, except on this night—the applause had finally stopped at the end of her show when someone tossed a penny on stage. The coin landed right at her feet. Never at a loss, Pearl just kicked it around for a second with her satin-covered toe, then with a mix of acid and oil said, "My mother always told me that only one kind of animal throws a scent."

In the cab going back to my hotel, a flood of memory took

me by surprise—and some painful personal moments came rushing into my head.

Getting into bed, I thought of Stella Brooks. I could see her the morning she took the Chinese horse from the Rubirosa party in Hollywood, and how the blame was unquestionably on me. Accepting a customer's invitation to continue a night's entertainment at his home was never one of my favorite pastimes. The night Peter Paanakker, a Beverly Hills art dealer, asked us to his house was a classic example. It had been Porfirio Rubirosa's idea not to end the evening—and it was very late when we finished at the Gala. Doris Duke was with him, though they had just been divorced. More champagne was in order—more and more—and there was plenty of it at the Paanakker's, an opulent place with a convenient baby grand in the living room. The venue was drinks, and a few songs to be supplied by the strolling players from the club, Robert Clary, Stella Brooks, and me. Clary was a willing guest, happy to stand up and perform. Then, without too much coaxing Stella took her turn. I was surprised, since she might easily take offense at her audience at the Gala. Often she'd do one song and be off the stage if she didn't like the reception from the crowd in the room. But obviously a less commercial atmosphere pleased her. She sang a few numbers, and then it was my turn. I tried to refuse politely, but Rubirosa wouldn't hear of it. "If you won't go to the piano, I will carry you!" he said, lifting me up and taking me across the room. I thought better of my bad manners and went ahead to sing two songs. Then we were on our way out—

"Those bastards weren't ready to lay any bread on us!" Stella said as we went through the hallway. Paanakker's mother collected Chinese jade, most of it displayed on a long table near the door, and Stella grabbed a T'ang—Ming—some dynasty or other—horse and stuffed it in her purse.

A call from Jim Dolan woke me the next morning. "Now,

Bobby, don't get excited," he began. "A Mr. Paanakker called. He says a priceless Chinese horse is missing from his mother's collection. What do you know about it?"

I told him what had happened, and he answered quickly. "Well, I'm not going to say who did the stealing. It was an accident, and he can stop by the club to pick up the horse."

That evening when she reported for work Stella brought back the horse, of course. And since she had taken it, she ought to take the blame, I thought. I never accepted Jim's flip reasoning—or the unspoken presumption that the black piano player had to be the thief.

I had been through this before, years ago at the Silhouette in Chicago when Bookie Levin called me into his office.

He closed the door behind us as soon as I walked in, something he had never done before. I wondered what momentous news was in store—and Bookie began looking embarrassed.

"You know, kid, how long we've known each other—what I have to say is very serious, and this is very hard for me."

"What are you talking about, Bookie?"

"Well, they're saying up on Howard Street that you stole a bottle of Scotch one night and went up to the Bar of Music to try to sell it to a customer."

"Stole a bottle of what—from where?"

"Now don't get excited. They say you took it from the storeroom at the Silhouette."

For the first time in my life I felt the breathlessness that came with rage. "I don't even know where the Scotch is stored. Besides, why would I want to steal a bottle and sell it? Who in hell told you this lie?"

"Now listen, kid, there are three sides to every story. Your side, the other guy's, and the truth."

I stuttered and stammered as though I'd been accused of murder—why would I steal when I didn't even like the taste of the stuff? It made no sense—I didn't need any extra cash. Why was I sitting there listening, trying to convince someone who had known me since I was twelve, who had given up his own bed for me? Then Bookie shifted gears—talking about new jobs, recording plans, Danville. . . . "How's your mother?" I went along with the conversation, but the reason for this call to the almighty throne room was painfully evident.

Now, all these years later, someone had thrown a penny at Pearl Bailey's feet. Geography did not matter one bit—no matter where we worked, prejudice still existed.

My contract at the Embassy was extended, and London was a happy place to be. An unexpected reunion of sorts took place when *Porgy and Bess* opened prior to a European and Russian tour. Cab Calloway, Leontyne Price and William Warfield were the stars, and I went to the theater with Pearl. No matter how many times I had seen it, the show always moved me. I was completely caught up in the familiar story—when Sportin' Life tempted Bess with the happy dust, I hoped she'd refuse him; when the first-act curtain came down I reached for my handkerchief the way I always did. Then later, as the entire company sang "I'm on My Way," Pearl turned to whisper to me, "Ain't nothin' in the world better than hearin' a bunch of colored folks sing."

London was still recovering from the long war; the shops and restaurants had a hard time getting the products needed for first-rate cooking—even eggs were hard to buy. The *Porgy* company became a welcome group at the Embassy, where the chefs managed to serve truly good food at supper after the show. Sometimes I went to Paris on my day off and came back with eggs and sweet butter. Leontyne and Bill were sharing a flat with another couple in the troupe, and Leontyne was quick to cook up Mississippi recipes for us. It was always the same pattern; when performers were a long way from home, eating out became a bore.

Bill had to leave to do a concert in New York, and before his departure he invited me to watch a rehearsal with his replacement. The action on stage was moving smoothly until the dense London fog that covered the city began to creep into the theater. Suddenly Catfish Row became all too real with a thick gray cloud rolling over the stage. Bill whispered that no one up there would be able to sing a note at the evening performance.

A few days later there was a mighty happy group at the Warfield flat when Bill returned from America with preparations for a feast—canned collard greens, black-eyed peas, food no one had seen for months and that Leontyne loved cooking.

One morning, at the registry office, Louis Bellson and Pearl were married. Marie Bryant came with her husband—what fun to have them in England. It seemed like ages since we were together at Nellie and Harold Brown's house, when Marie used to coach Betty Grable in her musical numbers at Fox. A sensational performer herself, Marie had danced in the Duke Ellington musical *Beggar's Holiday* and starred in the film *Jazz on a Summer's Day*, and here she was, living in London.

The Bellson Fan Club Jazz Band was playing when we came out of the building—the press loved it. The photographers were snapping away as we got into a limousine. Lunch was at Ziggy's, one of Pearl's favorite restaurants, and later the Colony hosted a gala in honor of the happy couple. No pennies were tossed on the stage that night. Bill sang "Some Enchanted Evening," Leontyne did "The Man I Love"—and I gave them "Gimme a Pigfoot."

One night before I went on, I heard a few of the fellows in the Cuban band talking outside my dressing room. Political discussions were rare at the club, and this conversation was very anti-American.

I thought they'd quit when I walked out the door. Instead it continued—and I told them that I was American, that what they were saying was not true—and impolite as well. What nationality did they think I was, anyway? One of them stopped me abruptly. "You defend a flag and a country that denies your people their rights? Your U.S. with its separate army, where a Negro cannot vote in the South. And how about your Senator Bilbo—he's a great patriot?" Then he went on about oil-guzzling big-business enterprises.

I had boasted about going to integrated schools in Danville, about driving my Cadillac in Hollywood. But my own success had nothing to do with what the Cuban musician was throwing at me. I asked myself how often Josephine Baker, the Duke, Louis Armstrong, and the Peters Sisters had heard all this, and were they caught without answers, as I was now?

Booking a plane to get back to Paris was easy, but when it might take off in the winter weather was another story. Blossom Dearie and Annie Ross were with me that day—Annie, Ella Logan's niece and the great jazz singer, was the third member of Lambert, Hendricks, and Ross. We waited for hours at the Kensington and High Street air station, drinking lukewarm tea, before we were bused out to Heathrow. And I saw Annie's passport, the name under her photograph—Annabelle Short! She told me the Shorts had been a renowned theatrical family in Scotland, and we roared at the possibility of being related.

In early January Paris was cold and very damp. Battles and I had found rooms on the Left Bank—the cost of gas to heat the place was as much as the rent. Not terribly spacious, but the apartment had many rooms, one so small it was more like a cell, but it had a wide window ledge where we chilled our champagne. We never went in there except for a bottle of wine.

With Blossom Dearie and Annie Ross in London.

Happily, John and I shared a love of extravagance. Determined to be more fluent in French, we had a tutor come to the apartment to give us lessons. By golly, we were going to speak this language as if it were our native tongue! We found a tailor who came to do personal fittings up the stairs of the ancient building on the Notre Dame des Champs off boulevard Raspail, the street where Ernest Hemingway had lived in the twenties. To us this was the height of style—and luxury! What bargains we found in the flea market. Steals we couldn't resist—things we could not live without. We would stop at the Ritz for a cocktail or at the Hotel Lotti. We met visiting Americans at the Plaza Athenée—where else!

Sometimes late at night we went to Jean's Intrigue for a nightcap, stepping through the front door off the street to make our way through a hole in the floor leading down a spiral staircase to the club. This was truly a cellar to end all cellars, but the jazz played there was exceptional. One night John, looking at the minuscule exit at the top of the stairs, said he wondered what the possible disaster might be if a fire ever broke out and we were with one of the very roly-poly Peters Sisters. "That's a very, very narrow space up there," John said. Happily, his hypothesis was never put to the test.

At Chez Inez one could have soul food, recipes served up by Inez Cavanaugh, who often broke out in a song. One of her special numbers was called "Everybody's Peein' in the Bidet 'Cause It's Cold in the WC." She paid particular attention to her poodle, Aillette, a white standard with claws painted bright red by Inez. Many a night the pampered Aillette would sit with her mistress on a chair of her own for the revue at the Folies-Bergère.

My resources were dwindling when the bleak Parisian winter hit us. I had no steady work schedule, and the few weeks in London hadn't left me with much. The flat was frigid and unheatable, and the insidious damp weather set off a series of nasty colds. Our landlord paid no attention to our requests for heat— or to pick up the trash, the rubbish that accumulated for so long, we thought it was enough to tempt every rodent up from the sewers of Paris.

With Machiavellian maneuvering, we arranged our getaway. We sent out the rugs and told the concierge they were going to the cleaners before the arrival of John's wife and daughter. They were indeed expected, but now Mrs. Battles was his ex-wife and coming for only a brief visit. When the great night came, we lowered bundles, parcel after parcel, out the fourth-floor windows to the sidewalk to waiting friends ready to load up a car with our accumulation of French bargains. I can't remember if we used rope or string or knotted bedsheets, but little by little we cleared out the apartment and made the trip across the Seine over to the Hotel de la Tremoille. We had duped our nasty landlord.

And it seemed far more practical to shift back to the Right Bank, close to the Lido for John and walking distance from my gig at the cellar called Spivy's East Side, where I earned 10,000 francs a night, which wasn't too bad.

Spivy was a dark woman with olive skin, black hair, and deep brown eyes. She was stout—does anyone still say "stout"?—and like all heavy performers, she moved lightly, easily, always wearing a long skirt and a tuxedo jacket with pailletted lapels in either red, black, or white. Simple—which was her total philosophy. She performed a wide range of obscure special material, most of it her own, some by Noel Coward, all of it risqué. Bawdy songs her audience knowingly sang along with her, laughing all the way. That is—when Madame Spivy chose to perform.

She had been quick to realize that American tourists liked to be with each other, and after midnight the club was packed with them, often outstanding performers. Her great trick was to darken the room before the spotlight caught her entrance. From the back would come her loud announcement: "Ladies and gentlemen, *mesdames et messieurs*, we are honored to have a star in our audience tonight, and I am sure he will treat us to a song or two—Mr. Dennis Day!" Or Lena Horne, or Pearl Bailey—whoever was in Paris that night. The shocked entertainer might stand up to be coaxed by the crowd to sing, but other times a performer quickly asked for the bill and beat a hasty and embarrassed retreat. Then Spivy simply had to go to the piano. Without any fuss, she got on with it.

She was a complete curiosity to the French—and they took her for a Negro. Once a reporter asked if she felt any discomfort being a Negress living in France, and Spivy took her time before responding. Then very seriously she replied, "No, my dear, absolutely none at all."

Of course, life was better when a new season brought more Americans, though I was impressing the French clients with my announcements and singing more and more in their language. The Gallic crowd ate it up. And I improved my accent.

February brought the fashion gang to swarm over the city for the spring collections: buyers, editors, and photographers, the dress designers. Lunch, drinks, and coffee at sidewalk cafes—and the best audience night after night at the club. I met Bill Blass. I was asked to do a sitting for *Vogue*. And I met George Huycke. Dapper and elegant with a whopping sense of humor. Strangers meeting him later always thought he was a famous actor and, I suppose, in many ways he really was. Our paths were destined to cross again and again.

And mail was coming from Hollywood with an offer to return to the Gala, followed by phone calls and telegrams, urging me to come back. The Gala had been bought by new people: Jimmy Hulse and Seymour Lazar. Jimmy was an old friend, and his partner-to-be was an attorney probably expecting a lark in the cabaret business. They were looking for an attraction to guarantee a steady clientele in their new enterprise—and I found myself thinking about it, considering what I might make, knowing that I surely could earn more than what I used to get. I would do a new act—make changes, use new ideas. Nothing specific, but it was clear that I had to do something different. And if I were to try something new, what better place than my old, familiar setting? I asked for $450 a week, and a deal was made.

I was going home!

One last week in Paris. One final lunch at Korniloff with blinis and caviar and vodka—then I was off to Orly.

I had cashed in the last of my traveler's checks, but there was a spiffy new topcoat on my back, custom-made by a Paris tailor. There were new suits in my bags—and a carton filled with perfume for Nellie Brown, who would be waiting with Harold when I stepped off the plane in Los Angeles.

The Coast
1953—55

From France to California was a considerable trip in 1953. Before departing I'd passed by the American hospital for the obligatory smallpox vaccination. The doctor gave me the vaccine in the thigh. "No point in having a sore arm if this gets worse on opening night," he said. An infection set in.

Covered with perspiration, and with the worst chills imaginable, I opened at the Gala, doing most of the new material I had learned in Paris and London. All in English. I wanted my audience to see I was still their local boy, who on foreign shores had made good. Not grand.

Just before my encore a voice rang out "Bobby, you've gotten so *thin!*" The woman at the front table made it sound as though I belonged in the nearest hospital—and from the way I felt, I might have been quick to agree with her. Was it because I was always walking in Paris and London, forgetting my California routine of jumping in the car to go to the corner drugstore, or did I look thin because of my new English suit—narrow trousers, narrow shoulders and lapels? Never mind which reason, tall and thin was swell with me.

Without thinking I began the encore, a light, beguinelike vamp, telling the room about the song. I had first heard it done by one of my idols, Henri Salvador; the lyric said that life, if approached sweetly and gently, can be managed despite all problems and worries. It was called "Doucement, Doucement." And I sang it in French.

"Fabulous," "marvelous," "wonderful"—the words were scattered like confetti in the cellar corner called my dressing room. After mopping myself and getting out of my wet, sweaty clothes, I listened to questions. "Only one song in French?" "Why not Charles Trenet?" Why this, why that, and I wondered—why had

Preceding page: With my sage mentor and manager, Phil Moore.

I come home? On the boulevard Raspail the leaves were whirling across the pavement—the gang from the Lido was probably gathering at a bar for a hot rum, for a *fine à l'eau*. My thigh was aching like mad.

And all of a sudden, the lightning flash. Here at home, they knew that I'd learned, I'd grown—and the audience was with me all the way. The club was packed every night for both shows, and the bar was jammed. Terrific—until the owners announced that they had made some serious miscalculations: their operating costs were too high no matter how good the business. This news was followed almost instantly by the return of my old nemesis, Jim Dolan. The old grudges, resentments, and panic returned, too, and I thought that aside from the sum in my pay envelope, *I* was right back where I started.

Jim Dolan was not happy about my salary, and it took only a few days for him to mount a campaign to whittle me down. Never mind—I had a contract, the sign on the roof had been reactivated, my name was up in lights again, and the place was doing capacity business night after night.

On a Saturday close to the end of my run, Hadda Brooks came in. She had a few hit records and on the strength of personal appearances around the country was rather a celebrity in our midst. Hadda was very pretty, with a low, husky voice—and she, too, played piano. It didn't take long for Dolan to go into action. He offered her a salary lower than mine—and had her appear as a surprise guest one night just before my last show. She took over and played past the legal closing time. By law and by contract I could not go on. I didn't—and the union backed me up.

A couple of nights later Hadda took my place. The union agreed to give Dolan a chance to pay me to the end of my contract before closing the place down, and another few weeks went by. Suddenly Dolan was gone. He had sold the Gala. The union stuck to their guns—and the new owners paid up.

Going to the union offices was quite a different matter now. In the old days, when I first went with Harold Brown, we walked into a wood-frame house on Central Avenue, the main drag in the black section of town. Back then the union had separate locals for white and Negro musicians in every town where contracts were registered and filed. This custom wasn't necessary in a town as small as Danville, but after working in Chicago, I always made a weekly trek to the local office to see that taxes and dues were paid on time. The people working in the offices were mostly former musicians who approved or disapproved contracts, collected dues, and made the rounds of the spots where black musicians were working. In my case, where a Negro player was hired "outside the jurisdiction"—which meant an area where blacks did not usually work—this produced a small amount of friction that was hardly discussed. But quite a few members of the colored and white locals were highly vocal about the separation. After all, in New York the American Federation of Musicians Local 802 had been integrated for years. There had been much pro and con about such a move, but most members were in favor of one union. The grumbling came mostly from officials who hadn't played their instruments professionally in years. A white agent had once said it was probably the doings of "a few Commies on your side and another few on our side." However, the differences were finally resolved in the old-fashioned way—a simple vote. And when I went to visit Local 47, it was on North Vine Street in Hollywood.

Not much later another Styne entered my life. This time it was a Stanley, son of composer Jule Styne. He was only twenty-three and full of ideas. Stanley thought I should be a stand-up performer, I ought to get away from the piano and play bigger rooms—like the ones in Las Vegas.

Stanley saw me making a commercial record as soon as possible. And with his father's help we could attract the Vegas big boys. Why not be right up there with the Johnny Rays, the Nat Coles? And he arranged a four-week booking at the Crescendo farther down the Strip, with the trio from the Gala to back me. Bass, piano, and guitar, just the security I needed, plus his cousin, Buddy Bregman, to do the orchestrations. I saw myself strolling around the room, using a hand mike and with an orchestra to provide the fanfare and bow music. I was going to do "No Other Love Have I," the new Rodgers & Hammerstein hit from *From Me and Juliet*.

The following day Hedda Hopper and Louella Parsons, rarely in accord, said I was sensational—it was sparkle time. Then on my third night megalaryngitis knocked me out. The doctor forbade me to go on—and ordered me to keep my mouth shut. For the next two weeks I scribbled notes day and night.

The rest of that summer was spent brooding. I had had a brilliant beginning—and then no middle, no end. Nerves had caused the laryngitis. Clearly my allergies were the result of nerves—the core, the kernel, the bane of the performer's being.

Over the years it happened again and again. Pull the string too tight and you break it; stretch the rubber band and it snaps. When the vocal chords are tampered with, a singer's demons emerge, whether he or she is singing at the Metropolitan or crooning in a saloon.

Stanley Styne and Buddy Bregman came by often to cheer me up, and how we talked! Plans, a grand strategy, because large acts were the latest thing in Las Vegas. Staged, directed, choreographed acts. I plunged into a new routine.

In the morning I trained at Lester Horton's dance classes. He was the master of modern style on the West Coast, an influence on many of the great names in dance, Alvin Ailey and Carmen de Lavallade among them.

Afternoons I spent with Alex Romero, who was staging the act. That he had come from Metro to work with Bobby Short couldn't have pleased me more—and he made my self-consciousness vanish when he got me away from the piano. He knew how to accent a lyric with a movement, to point up a rhythm without making me into a production number.

Details fell into place quickly—Buddy was doing the orchestrating and arranging, Stanley had gone to Associated Booking, and Joe Glaser was ready to line up the engagements. One thing was certain: none of my old material was going to be used. All of this was going to be new—new—*new*!

Somehow I seemed to have forgotten Dwight Fiske's voice whispering in my ear years before. How young I must have been when the granddaddy of saloon singers gave me his advice: "Never leave the piano, Bobby."

During rehearsals I realized that amplification was going to present a problem. We were off to San Diego, to a club called Tops with a sizable dance floor—and though the orchestra consisted of only eight pieces, I knew a mike was necessary. But what kind? No overhead equipment was available, no standing mike was going to work. Then Harold Brown came to my rescue with a specialist in the then new wireless microphones.

The act was set. Buddy Bregman was going to lead the band, and I bought slate-gray evening trousers and black patent shoes to wear with an open-neck evening shirt and a cummerbund of bright colors. I was ready for my star turn.

I don't know how I got through it. I had been full of pizzazz when I began. Three numbers, all of them stand-up, then an exit, then back on stage and to the piano. I had heard polite applause when I went off and cheering as I sat down. Was this the reason they had come—to see me sitting at a piano? Finally it was over. Or almost over—because the pals came backstage. The loyal boosters, the close friends, the naysayers—with their constructive criticism and their limited praise.

The week wore on. Sometimes the new-technology mike

worked just fine, other times it was as temperamental as a diva and refused to work at all. Buddy was gone after opening night, and the bandleader put his musicians through the numbers without attention to tempo or cues.

Yale Kahn, who owned Tops, didn't tell me that my second week was to be a split one. Shelley Winters came in before her date in Vegas to try out her new act, which went very smoothly. Every bit of it effective—and slick. Slick hair, slick saloon gown, slick arrangements, and a monologue from *A Place in the Sun* with the score from the movie playing behind her.

The L.A. gang came down in full force—including Stanley's father, Jule. Cross the fingers, I said to myself, get through it. I had cut the nonsense out of the act, what I thought did not work. I had enough confidence and experience, I kept saying to myself, to carry it off. And then I was out there on the floor, opening my mouth for the first words of "From This Moment On." Into a dead mike. A mike that stayed dead while I belted the songs as loudly as my lungs would allow.

The success of my desperate shouting can be measured by Yale Kahn's backhanded compliment after the performance. "Bobby," he said, "you don't leave anything at all to the imagination of the audience—every word is demonstrated neatly by your gestures when you're out there." Some compliment—I could have killed him.

No staggering offers came from the magic oasis out on the Mojave Desert, no big Las Vegas contracts were waved in my face. But we had made my first record in Los Angeles, and Stanley had set the release date—now the road to stardom led up north.

First to Santa Barbara, to a sleazy room attached to a motel, sharing the spot with a lady called La Contessa.

Then to Portland, the Clover Club, where there were four musicians to play orchestrations written for a twelve-piece band.

For some reason it worked out rather well. A redhead named Phyllis Inez was on the bill, and we worked out a show with Blue Angel style and intimacy. My record was heard on the radio quite a lot up there—and after I sang "Le Metro Rumba" one night, a customer asked if I really sang it in French, or had I just made up those words to sound French.

From Portland we went to Spokane, to a staid place with polite atmosphere, run like a private club, where no man off the Spokane streets seemed to be welcome. Opening night Phyllis had barely enough applause to warrant a bow. And for me it was no-go from the start. I belted and mugged, I pounded and shouted, but the guests were unmoved. My fastest-ever exit set us off into gales of laughter in our dressing area. We had come only a few miles farther north, but more than the temperature was icy. And it did not change all week. On the last night I charged up the crowd enough to give them one extra song—and when I was finished the orchestra leader walked off stage to talk to me. "Well, now don't you feel better after that stirring ovation?" For Spokane it was apparently pretty hot stuff.

It was the beginning of September when I got back to Los Angeles, and at last an offer came in from Las Vegas. My used Olds needed repairs, and I was broke. Now the Browns came to my rescue once again—this time it was Nellie who asked her sister for a loan. The car was fixed, so I put twenty-five dollars in the pocket of my jeans and got into the Olds to head out to the Mojave Desert.

Playing a lounge in Vegas presented problems after the elaborate schemes of Stanley Styne, all the work that Romero and Bregman had done. To sit at the piano might be okay, but to fit my newly staged, watered-down stand-up act into a small playing area was no easy feat. Fortunately the sound of slamming slot machines and the noise of the gambling tourists did not interfere at the Last Frontier. The lounge was separate from the open gambling area—

unlike the other hotels where the big "name" acts played in the main rooms while the lounge provided nonstop entertainment amid the clamor of the game playing. And for a six-week contract at seven hundred smackers a week I was more than willing to muddle through.

And what a break to find superior backup musicians waiting when I arrived—bass, drums, and piano who instantly grasped what I was doing. We had a short rehearsal, since most of the parts were for my almost obsolete stand-up act, but we were able to patch together enough to see us through the opening. By now I knew that any performance itself is almost always better than rehearsal, because the crowd tells you where the slow and the bad spots are. I had learned that the energy of the audience was what pointed me in the best direction.

January on the desert brought sunny days, and the snow-capped mountains in the distance made it as picturesque as I had been told—near perfect atmosphere.

But no one had talked about the other atmosphere—the racial one that existed as if it were still the Dark Ages and not 1954. A little like those dark-tunnel rides at a carnival, with an unexpected surprise waiting at every abrupt turn.

Sammy Davis Jr. came in to follow James Melton, the Metropolitan Opera tenor, who was headlining at the Frontier and knocking them dead with his rendition of "Short'nin' Bread." I ran into Sammy on his way to a rehearsal, and he asked me where I was staying. I told him the motel that Herman Hover, the entertainment manager, had booked for me was pretty good; it was only across the street and down a way. Sammy had to run, but he wished me luck, saying that he was living in the colored section of town. It had never occurred to me that white hotel owners took no responsibility about first-class accommodations for stars of another color. Well, Herman had done almost right by me then. I couldn't have a room at the Last Frontier, but at least he had arranged for me to be within walking distance.

The motel was comfortable enough, and the young couple who ran it liked the contact with show people. They clearly felt no animosity toward a black presence in their midst. I had one meal a day there in a dining room with a square counter that was good for eating alone—but a snack at four in the morning had to be found somewhere else. Early on I went to the Chuck Wagon buffet for late gamblers at the hotel, until one night a New York showgirl named Jean Malone, who had looked me up, came to join me there. Her platinum hair and alabaster complexion may have been the reason I was summoned to the manager's office to hear that I was not to let such a meal happen again. Was I south of the Mason-Dixon line? I wanted to know. "Nothing to do with management, you understand. . . ." I listened to the old excuse. "But we have to respect our discriminating clientele."

I realized then why Sammy was living across town. I knew that Steve Gibson and his Red Caps had to dress in a trailer brought in just for them. To allow these fellows in the same quarters as the white performers was . . . what? Contaminating. Even Damita Jo had to dress in a trailer.

And Nat Cole said that such goings-on might hurt his ability to perform. He laughed when he said it, but he was dead serious—and what happened? Not a bloody thing.

Lena Horne stood alone; she had landed the unheard-of privilege of staying at the Sands Hotel. But when I told her I wanted to see her show, she was quick to interrupt me. "Just wait until I call Jack Entratter and you can sit at his table. I know how difficult things can be in this damned town."

The Golden Slipper was designed as an old-style saloon with sawdust floors and gaslight chandeliers, without any formality. "Nothing doing," the bartender said when I went in with a group of white friends early one morning after work. "We don't serve colored in here."

At the Desert Inn Hotel in Palm Springs with songwriter Jimmy Van Heusen and singer-of-the-century Frank Sinatra.

I'd been asked to join a friend at the Sands lounge for a drink, and the manager made it quite clear he was not at all pleased. I hoped he'd be off duty the next time—but his shift was unpredictable—and if he was on, I was not allowed in.

Marilyn Maxwell had come to town to follow Sammy Davis Jr. in the main room of the Frontier. A tough act to follow, but Marilyn came through with a knockout performance of her own. She had been a firm fan at the Gala, and after she finished her act, scrubbed clean of makeup, she often stopped at the Lounge for a nightcap. Where to go if we were hungry when I finished my last set was the problem . . . until it became a kind of game for us to play. We knew which manager at what lounge was biased enough to stop us from entering, and we soon discovered who else there might be to let us in for a bite to eat. If we saw the villain was on duty, we'd move along to some other place. It was almost a joke to run around town in the small hours of the morning, tempting the gods of prejudice—to see where we might upset the status quo.

Helen Gallagher was opening at the Thunderbird, where she was staying, and Phil Moore, who had staged her act, was at my motel. Talking to Phil was effortless; our conversation was in a kind of shorthand, almost as if he knew what I was thinking before I told him. I had barely touched on my supposed stand-up act and the frustrations that came with it when he looked me square in the eye and asked, "What do you *want* to do, son?" and then said, "If you'd like to talk more, I'll be on the Coast in a couple of weeks, maybe we can get together." Funny, how the West Coast was always referred to as "the *Coast*."

The morning was warm when I packed up the Olds and took off for Los Angeles. I knew what was ahead of me beyond the desert highway. With Phil's prodding I had made up my mind to get out of the contracts with Associated Booking and Stanley Styne, who would be the first to understand. It had been an experience—an instructive one. But, for sure, a big, flashy act was not for me. Orchestrations and wireless mike, cummerbunds and slate-gray trousers, were as instantly distant as the dry desert disappearing behind me.

A small, tufted room with a grand piano and a reliable sound system. That was what I needed—along with the respect and attention I received as an intimate singer and pianist.

Nothing here at the Carlyle will ever remind me of Palm Springs, though I can still hear Jimmy Van Heusen offering me work there after I finished a job in Los Angeles. And a job at the Desert Inn along the main drag of that little California town could in no way compare with the wasteland of Nevada that I had recently left behind me. Palm Springs epitomized swank and luxury—in other words, money with none of the razzmatazz of Las Vegas.

Jimmy, a celebrated songwriter, had a pleasant and generous personality and the world's most wide-open smile. I was put up at a comfortable motel with a swimming pool. Every amenity of the Desert Inn was available to me, including their pool. And on the grounds I had the run of Jimmy's cottage—with yet another pool. The room at the Desert Inn was spacious, and there was a beautiful clientele of beautiful people on hand every evening. Writers and directors, producers and actors, all of whom came down from Hollywood. I found myself playing to Doris Day, Cesar Romero, Marion Davies (and her new, protective husband, Horace Brown), Broderick Crawford, the ravishing Lisa Ferraday, and Jimmy's best friend, Frank Sinatra. It was a warm, infor-

mal way of life, and I had the attention of my peers
while I worked. This was the Hollywood I had imagined
a dozen years earlier when I left Omaha. Now on my
nights off I was in the group at Sinatra's house, feasting
on his food, all of us singing for one another—Frank,
Maria and Nat Cole—even Jimmy's miniature poodle,
programmed to howl at the mention of Hoagy
Carmichael's name—Hoagy lived just across the way
and before I left, the dog was in training to respond to
the first notes of "Stardust."

I was driving a new Thunderbird and thinking that
I was truly playing with the big boys, that life in such a
rarefied atmosphere could go on forever. Then Phil
Moore called.

"Robin, a new room is opening at the Beverly Hotel
in New York!" He had been searching for a Manhattan
spot for months while I did the Palm Springs gig. Now
he had found one.

New York
1956

Diagonally across from the Waldorf on Lexington Avenue stood the respectable, stolid Beverly Hotel. Richard Maidman, the owner, wanted to liven things up, and he turned the mezzanine into a cabaret called the Beverly Club.

As soon as the announcements appeared, old friends like Jean and Bob Bach, Dorothy and Dick Kollmar, were calling for reservations. After all the splendid publicity Dorothy had given me, it was a very special sight to see her smiling with pleasure the first night they came in. New Yorkers, the true ones, were now an admiring sea of faces sitting only a few feet from my piano. The Bachs brought John Hammond and his witty, knock-out wife, Esme.

John Hammond, sprung from the old New England family, was the great authority on jazz and blues, on what was the best and the most *now* in music. What a renegade he was, coming out of that straitlaced background to discover Count Basie in Kansas City and bring him to New York, to be the man who talked Barney Josephson into hiring Billie Holiday for the downtown Cafe Society.

I can still see John Hammond at a music publisher's office in Chicago when I was no more than twelve. I played the piano for him—played, hell: I did an audition. In those days I was used to hearing "He's a darling," "the best," "a genius." But not from John Hammond. He said I had talent, but why was a boy my age working? Bookie told him my talent made money. Mr. Hammond said I should forget about work, that I ought to be studying music, learning to read notes, and that eventually I could be really outstanding. Now, more than twenty years later, John Hammond had competed with Ahmet Ertegun to buy my first LP for his Vanguard label. And here he was, in the audience.

Preceding page: Bobby Short at the Blue Angel with Ann Newburger in the background.

Naturally, the Erteguns came in. Ahmet had a vested interest, since it was his company, Atlantic, that released the record I had made with Phil Moore.

Phil was meticulous in planning with his partner, Allen Best. And overseeing the ads and the press coverage was Ruth Cage. Ruth, my first crush, who had made a career for herself as a publicist in the city she had dreamed about when we'd first met at the Browns' in Hollywood.

After the opening I felt that at last I was at home in New York, those early days at the Blue Angel in 1945 only a dim memory. Richard Maidman gave me a two-room suite at the hotel, and between shows I had friends filling my living room. And after my second show we could rush to Tony's to hear Mabel Mercer. Or go down to the Village to see Jimmy Daniels at Bon Soir.

I had met Jimmy during that initial gig at the Blue Angel. I first saw him walking down the aisle at the theater one night when I had a seat in the balcony, the best that I could afford back then. I watched him with his friends, all of them well dressed, but Jimmy the most impeccable. A few weeks later I learned that he had manners to match—the impression was indelible. He had a modest, casual kind of charm and perfect diction. That was the night I had gone to Jock's Place, his club uptown in Harlem.

Now he ran Bon Soir, the club down the stairs on West Eighth Street, singing with chubby Mae Barnes and the Three Flames, the trio that featured Tiger Haynes on guitar. I soon found that Jimmy was an expert cook, staging at-home parties with the same style with which he ran Bon Soir.

Tad Adoue was someone else with his own special flair. A native of Dallas, Tad had not only the accent, but the curiosity and enthusiasm that seemed inherent to Texans. He had wanted to be an architect; instead he became a low-key patron of the theater and an insightful art collector. He had a crazy affection for cotton bandannas—red ones, blue ones, whatever colors he found in Army and Navy Surplus stores or shops selling western gear. He wore them constantly—around his neck by day with a pair of jeans and a sport coat . . . in the breast pocket of a suit by night. An idea too good not to copy in the pocket of my dinner jacket before I went on at the Beverly Club.

Marguerite Lampkin had been a customer at the Gala, bright and pretty and with a Louisiana accent as strong as Tad Adoue's Texas twang. She was always traveling, but one night she was in New York meeting me when I came off stage—the voice of the bayou singing my praises. "You-ah just mahvelous, isn't it gra-and that you-ah heah in New York!" We talked for a minute, kissed quickly, and then she was off with her date. Only a minute later she was rushing back to catch me before I went upstairs to my room. "Baah—by," she was squealing with excitement, "the duchess is coming in to hear you!" I didn't have to ask which duchess. Everybody knew the Windsors were in New York; the columns constantly reported every lunch, dinner, and party given for them. In a second the maître d' was leading them to a special table set up close to the piano.

The duchess was the only woman in the party, clearly enjoying the admiration of the three men at the table—but not for a moment neglecting to pay special attention to her husband.

During the show one of the men lit a cigarette, the glow lighting their table for an instant. And I had a momentary movie-fan flashback. Here was I, the kid from Danville, Myrtle Short's boy, playing for the most famous royal couple in the world.

They wanted to meet me when the show was over. The duke, a keen amateur drummer, was the first to extend his hand. "Mr. Short, we loved the drums that roll before you come on and when you take your bow." Phil Moore had dreamed up that idea, and I knew he'd be tickled at the royal approval.

The next morning the news was in every paper. I had received a regal thumbs-up. The rush was on to see what the Windsors were so excited about.

The Bachs were doing personal publicity, too—sending friends in every night from their world of television and radio. Carol McCallson trumpeted the word through the fashion crowd. Carol had been spreading good news about me since her days of commuting from Glendale to see me at the Haig. With a sense of style as sharp as her sense of humor, she had moved from California model to Manhattan model—and what a marvelous reunion we had.

In came Arlene Francis and Martin Gabel, the George Axelrods, Nat and Maria Cole, Jule Styne, Betty Comden, and Faye Emerson, who asked to interview me on her daytime show at NBC. Faye was good-looking and intelligent, an easygoing hostess with her husband, Skitch Henderson, at their house in the East Sixties and a happy companion at P. J. Clarke's when I'd meet her after work for a hamburger and a drink.

And in the midst of the sell-out audiences I saw Dorothy Kilgallen—beaming with what I took to be absolute motherly pride. In her way, Dorothy was responsible for most of the success I was enjoying.

Before leaving California, I'd had a tailor make me a few dinner jackets, and I wanted some special finishing touches for those beautifully tailored Harry Cherry suits. I'd noticed a jacket William Helburn wore when he was photographing me for some magazine, a tie-silk lining flashing when his coat was open. A few weeks into the engagement one of my fans assured me, "Bobby, your red silk lining is the most far-out thing in New York!"

One day Eddie Collins called from MCA, asking if I'd consider a three-week revival of *Kiss Me Kate* at City Center. Burt Shevelove was directing; he had been into the club and thought I'd

be dynamite in the part of the valet, Paul, who opened the second act with "Too Darn Hot." And Shevelove had said that no audition would be necessary.

Once I had auditioned for Cole Porter himself, and I did not get the job. The part was meant for a dancer, so I went back to the Gala to sing "Too Darn Hot" every night. Now I was asked to be at the first day of rehearsal—just show up, Eddie had said.

"I'm not a dancer," I told Burt the first morning.

"So?" He shrugged. "You can move, can't you?" I nodded. "Well then, the job is yours."

I learned a few simple steps, I mastered the dialogue and sang the song. Listening to every word was my very nervous understudy, Arthur Mitchell, who had told Burt that while I could sing and *maybe* could dance, he could dance but he *certainly* couldn't sing.

Rehearsals flew by. We opened and had good notices. I'd had no idea what "acting" was. But with Burt's help, I had pulled it off. On the last day of rehearsal he had asked me to sing my song while he sat in the back of the house to be sure that I could be heard. Up there on the vast stage of City Center, I was without my microphone and determined to project without straining. After all, I had worked long years on big cabaret floors without any acoustic help. Why not here? I was not about to disappoint Burt Shevelove—and after reading the notices, I knew I hadn't let him down. In this company of Broadway pros I was not about to let anyone down—I simply *had* to prove myself.

Kitty Carlisle was starring in the revival with David Atkinson, and her husband, Moss Hart, often dropped in at rehearsals. Of course I was eager to make an impression on the man who had worked with my favorite composers, Berlin and Porter and Kurt Weill, who had written and directed so many legendary Broadway musicals. He was rehearsing his new show, *My Fair Lady*, with a score by Lerner & Loewe, and I found him supportive, kind, and easy to talk to.

Ruth Cage worked overtime—she saw to the interviews, the television appearances. And, perhaps because of her, my stay at the Beverly was extended.

Eighteen weeks—it had been freezing when we opened in February, now the streets were beginning to steam up as New York's sweltering summer began. In spite of the city's blistering heat, I was a New Yorker now. The city was home to me—and I was most definitely a part of its irresistible tempo, its seductive pace. But, worry wart that I was, I wondered what came next.

One sunny July morning I went to Phil Moore's office. I

began tentatively, suddenly nervous about bringing up the future, the inevitable question. Phil leaned back on his big chair, puffing on his pipe with pleasure before he smiled at me. "Robin, I'm just gonna sit back and watch the good things happen."

I had dreams of instant fame and fortune. What I had yet to learn was not to count my chickens.

New York
1956—65

Winter came quickly that year, and a job came, too—not the most elegant of gigs, but a job. In one of the many East Side brownstones that had housed so many families in another less hectic and far more innocent time. The Red Carpet's main attraction was the lineup of hookers at the front bar before you stepped into the main room, where there was a grand piano. The owner, Freddy Jacobs, was a likable fellow in his mid-forties, and I got the picture pretty fast. He was hoping someone new playing in his room would clear out the clientele at the bar. I remembered that in Paris quite a few girls came to see me, and what an attractive picture they made when they stood at the Mars, with their mint frappés resting on the tin counter. It seemed to me there were a few over at Spivy's, too—relaxing in her Parisian cellar, perhaps hoping to find some truly romantic interlude in the ambivalent atmosphere Madame presented.

I spent eight months at the Red Carpet. I don't know what happened to the bar lineup, whether the ladies changed their style of dress or whether they forsook Freddy's for a more workable bistro. But soon the faces I saw both at the bar and in the room were familiar. The crowd from the Beverly had followed me. The New York columnists had begun to note that I was out on the town a lot with Korby Pleasant. Both pretty *and* smart, she'd come East to manage Jax, an upscale sportswear shop for women.

One night stands out distinctly. I was well into the middle of my act when wisps of smoke came streaming out of the kitchen. The room was packed, the audience receptive, and the roiling smoke was increasing. I went on playing and singing, repeating to myself that the show must go on. It seemed that the outpour from the kitchen might suffocate us any minute, when a crew of firemen arrived through the front door and marched to the back of the

Preceding page: Singing and dancing with Danny Meehan and Dodie Goodman in Ben Bagley's Cole Porter revue.

193

room. On I went, finishing one song, starting another. The smoke subsided. The firemen, job done, made their exit—and the crowd gave them a round of applause loud enough to satisfy any star performer. Not one customer had panicked, no one attempted to leave the club, and I had gone on without missing a beat.

That spring, when it was time for me to leave, Freddy cancelled my bar tabs and gave me a gold watch. I wondered if it was a token of appreciation for panic prevention or for turning the Red Carpet into a smart East Side club instead of the local hooker bar.

Off Park avenue, east of Madison, west of Lexington, just off Fifth—club after club, saloon after saloon. Past the bar and up a staircase, through the lobby and down the steps. One room, then another and another. Job followed job—a long engagement or a short one, then a weekend spot, then maybe only one night.

Le Cupidon was one of the down-the-stairs places, east of Madison. I sang "I Left My Hat in Haiti." The calypso craze had hit New York; Caribbean was in. And out of a clear sky, Phil Moore had a call from Herbert Jacoby—with an offer for me to come back to the Blue Angel. For a thousand dollars a week.

Bart Howard had taken over the reins as emcee at the Angel. Composer of some wonderful songs—"Fly Me to the Moon" was one—when we first met he was Mabel Mercer's accompanist at Tony's. Now he introduced the acts, played during the intervals, and moved to the outside bar to play again later in the evening. I never felt that I raised the roof in the Angel's cozy, well-upholstered inner sanctum. But taking over up front made a difference. Eadie and Rack had been playing the bar, so had Portia Nelson, Martha Davis, and Billy Roy. Enid Mosier had brought her calypso combo in. There in the barroom I worked without a microphone. It was hell on the vocal chords, but the audience reaction was wonderful. I felt like the king of Fifty-fifth Street when I worked at the Angel, which I did off and on until 1963.

Opening Tuesday, November 14

in the lounge of

The Blue Angel

152 East 55th Street

BOBBY SHORT

nightly 10:30 to closing, except Saturday

Cocktails Sunday   5 to 8 p. m.

For reservations call Dario   PL 3-5998

In and out of clubs. Keep the image and maintain the salary, Phil Moore said, and he constantly shopped around. I landed on Second Avenue—the Living Room. With worn-down banquettes and a stifling atmosphere, it was not the place I'd come to New York to play. Rogers "Popsie" Whittaker of *The New Yorker* refused even to list it in the magazine until the chums came to cheer me on, and then he changed his mind.

Another summer and I was back on the Sunset Strip at the Interlude, sharing the bill with Shelley Berman, whose admirers arrived just before he went on. Often I played to a half-empty room. Or I was costarring with the Dancing Waters—a happening that took place on the terrace, with music synchronized to complex light effects and lots of dazzling fountains. Then Lenny Bruce. Some people found him abrasive, many more were enchanted—including me.

There was Billy's, on the outskirts of Cleveland, then back to New York, to the Weylin on Madison, where Cy Walter had played—the summit of hotel bars along the avenue. The hotel had

On top of the town at the piano in front of one of my favorite backdrops. Who could ask for anything more?

become an office building, but the old cachet remained. The contract was for twenty weeks, the salary was just fine. Atlantic Records made my first "live" recording during three exuberant nights with good audiences. Then, without warning, the room shut down. Business problems had forced the owner out.

My record album was released by the Erteguns, *Bobby Short on the East Side*, with me on the cover, stepping out of Ahmet's Rolls-Royce, a liveried chauffeur at the car door and Grand

Central Station behind me. The essence of New York, urbane and stylish. And I was out of a job.

Until Boston. In a jazz club called Storyville, where I succeeded Thelonious Monk. Very prestigious company. It had been the brainstorm of George Wein, one of Neshui Ertegun's friends and a pianist himself. Why not let the local jazz buffs have a glimpse of Bobby Short? he said.

And on East Fifty-second Street, the Arpeggio opened. I was with jazz greats Roy Eldridge, then Barbara Carroll—and two months flew by with a great crowd coming in—Joan Crawford in white mink, Hazel Scott, looking terrific and apologizing for her unprofessional behavior at the Mars in Paris years ago.

The 1960s rolled in, and Herbert Jacoby wanted me back on Fifty-fifth Street once more, in the Blue Angel bar, backed by drums and bass. I had to do one performance after the first show in the back room was over, and again after the second. One night my old fans, the Windsors, were ushered through to the inner room by a too eager maître d'. And after only a minute or two they were led back to the bar, to a banquette close to me at the piano. My good-luck lady Dorothy Kilgallen was there to watch the scene, and the papers picked up the item. It did not hurt one bit.

And the sight of Vivien Leigh and Terence Rattigan sitting together didn't hurt, either. Or Leonard Bernstein, standing at the bar one night, asking for the obscure songs he loved to hear. We made a game of it and the crowd ate it up.

Jacoby asked for a Sunday afternoon cocktail performance,

and the booming bar business helped offset the waning enthusiasm for entertainers working the main room. Young talents like Carol Burnett and Peter, Paul and Mary, Dorothy Loudon, and Barbra Streisand were being lured away by bigger money in television. Cabaret was losing its following. Carl Van Vechten and Fania Marinoff appeared one day—the superb portrait photographer who captured the twenties in his pictures and novels, with his wife, who had been a silent screen actress. What better couple to remember other times and other rooms, when nightlife in the city was thriving.

And what other place represented that other time more than the truly beautiful Cafe Ambassador off the lobby in the late, lamented Ambassador Hotel on Park Avenue. Grand and stylish, and perhaps not understood by its new corporate owner. The Sheraton chain replaced managers almost weekly, and no concepts were ever defined. The hotel didn't last long.

Off to Fifty-second Street again—just east of Fifth Avenue. And of all the clubs, the Caprice stands alone, perhaps because I was a partner in the venture. Herbert Jacoby had always wanted to own what he termed an "haute cuisine" restaurant. He found a rich friend who agreed with him and talked me into what he called a "can't miss" endeavor.

It was a starry opening, but a gig in Chicago two weeks earlier had taken its toll. With a tough sound system set up for jazz instrumentals, I had been singing too loudly out there—and I knew it wasn't called the Windy City for nothing. Everything about the fierce Chicago climate got to me. My allergies were in full bloom. And opening the Caprice with laryngitis and a packed room was a killer. My faithful fans were on hand plus a crowd of luminaries—including Sinatra, who, after seeing the first show, came back to warn me. "Either you take care of that throat, Bobby, or all you'll be able to do is hum."

Le Caprice—how aptly we had named it. Where one could

eat wonderful food, instead of concentrating on drinks and the performer at the piano! Despite Jacoby's pie-in-the-sky philosophy, our smart little haute cabaret didn't make it—not for more than a year and three months. And before I knew it, my savings were gone. Then I truly understood what being on your uppers meant.

I had to pay for my studio at Carnegie Hall, with no work, not even a recording deal, in sight—if a private party came along, I grabbed it, a one-night gig out of town gave me enough to cover the rent.

At the Square East down in the Village, Ben Bagley had been successful with a Cole Porter revue. He was putting together a second version, and he wanted me in it. A fair run, then it was over.

One evening I walked across Fifty-sixth Street and stopped at a place that had just opened. L'Intrigue—with Jimmy Daniels working the downstairs room and a spot available—where else— up a flight of stairs. The owner made me an offer, and I jumped at the chance. I worked the lights, I seated the customers, I'm not sure I didn't check the coats. But I was able to pay my bills.

Besides nerves, all performers carry a common cross called insecurity. New sounds and new faces were taking center stage. There were new places to go—Filmore East, Studio 54. The Beatles and their contemporaries broke all records on the music charts. And I began to wonder if the world that was listening to Bob Dylan's "Mr. Tambourine Man" or his "Blowin' in the Wind" wanted to hear Cole Porter, Gershwin, or Rodgers & Hart. Maybe my kind of music was old hat, passé. Maybe I was, too.

The tone of nightlife seemed to be changing everywhere else as well. Around that time Victor Lowndes and Hugh Hefner asked me over to London to open their new Playboy club. There in Park Lane, a penthouse flat overlooking Hyde Park was part of the deal. Sinatra's "Strangers in the Night" and a new soft-rock version of the old Jerome Kern favorite "The More I See You" were at the top of the charts. I had a swell ten weeks in all in London that summer, seeing lots of old friends and collecting, among other things, a Saville Row tailor before returning to the New York doldrums.

I didn't recognize then that the glamorous nightlife of the fifties and early sixties was history, that it was not lack of talent or charisma that attracted only small audiences made up of my ever-loyal fans. Times had changed, people were not going to supper clubs the way they used to. Business was off everywhere. The days—or rather, the nights—of staying out late, of nightclubbing and pub crawling, of meeting the milkman on the way home, were over.

There's almost no set Beverly, Robb, and I do in this room that doesn't include some Gershwin. Tonight it's "Things Are Looking Up"—and Ira Gershwin's lyrics sound almost eerily prescient when I think about what came after my gig at L'Intrigue.

I felt I had hit a dead end. But Gershwin's lyrics say something else:

> Bitter was my cup
> But no more will I be the mourner
> For I've certainly turned the corner
> Things are looking up. . . .

Even though I didn't know it at the time, looking up was indeed the way things were.

New York
1966–68

One night a face from the past appeared at L'Intrigue. Allen Best had been Phil Moore's partner, and he said the Living Room, where I'd worked earlier, wanted me back. No rock and roll over at Danny Siegal's place on Second Avenue. Never mind that there were two floors to play and the place was tantamount to being tacky. They had a strong clientele—and I could bring my following.

The Living Room worked, it worked very well for a long time. Helped along handsomely by a press agent who arrived via my old friend Ruth Cage. Betty Lee Hunt knew the business inside out, and she was familiar enough with my work to know that a song I sang was a great idea for a party. "Come to Bobby Short's Motion Picture Ball," read the invitations. A Joe Eula sketch of me fronted our mailing piece and was plastered all over town. Come as your favorite movie star. Come as yourself if you are a star! And they came—Liza Minnelli and Peter Allen, Joan Bennett, Maureen Stapleton, and most everyone working on Broadway. Angela Lansbury and Rex Reed played hosts, Tallulah Bankhead arrived in a dark dress with a sash draped across her front that announced she was Bette Davis. The party was a smash, as happy and wacky as the song

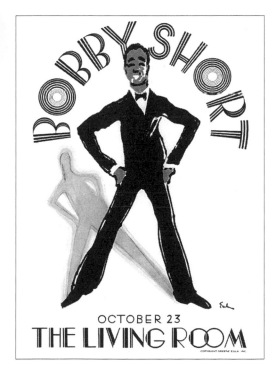

BOBBY SHORT

OCTOBER 23
THE LIVING ROOM

Preceding page: With the inimitable Tallulah Bankhead playing Bette Davis.

On the beach at Acapulco.

that inspired it. The Living Room was making money. I was in business again.

The following winter I was staying with Francine and Douglas McKelvey in Acapulco. The McKelveys were fans who had become good buddies, and their Georgian house on Cape Cod had been a God-sent refuge for me on many summer weekends. Douglas was a staunch Republican who hooted when their baronial house facing the bay in Hyannis Port was pointed out by tourist boats as the Kennedy compound, which was located almost next door and was far less imposing. Knowing how much I needed a rest, they had suggested that I come visit them in Mexico. One afternoon a call came through from George Wein, now a jazz entrepreneur. He had a wild notion—would I be interested in doing a New York concert with Mabel Mercer in May, at Town Hall? Would I? You bet!

And when May came, every seat in Town Hall was sold out—the management had to put chairs on the stage to handle the overflow. Ahmet and Neshui Ertegun never missed a beat: the concert was recorded for Atlantic, and a questionnaire touting the album was in every program. People *did* want to hear the old songs. And Mabel, with her always uncanny intuition, suggested that we finish with a duet of "Feelin' Groovy." The Simon and Garfunkel hit gave an added fillip to our performance and gave me one more reason to marvel at Mabel.

Stephane Grappelli, the great jazz violinist, once told me that his biggest thrill as a musician came when he accompanied Mabel at the piano. This was in the early thirties in Paris, when she was on the bill at Chez Florence. There the music went on until dawn, and Grappelli not only adored working with Mabel, but got a welcome respite from playing the violin hour after hour. She sang in her sweet, soft voice, scorning a microphone but sometimes using a tiny megaphone to sing into the ear of a patron without the distraction of other chattering customers. What an idea.

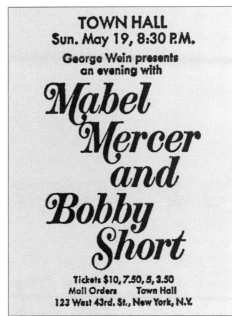

TOWN HALL
Sun. May 19, 8:30 P.M.

George Wein presents
an evening with

*Mabel
Mercer
and
Bobby
Short*

Tickets $10, 7.50, 5, 3.50
Mail Orders   Town Hall
123 West 43rd. St., New York, N.Y.

Mabel was the daughter of an English-Welsh woman and a black man. Her father died before she was born, her mother traveled the variety circuit. Raised in a convent, from early adolescence she had been a member of a touring vaudeville troupe, and she must have profited mightily from her early association with Florence Embry Jones, one of the first black women to leave the United States for foreign shores after the First World War. Madame Florence dazzled her clients with a splendid wardrobe and her own particular way with a song, until drugs and alcohol cut short what might have been a brilliant career. At Chez Florence, Mabel began to shape the repertoire she would continue to sing for the rest of her career, from revues like *In Dahomey* and *Blackbirds*. No one but Mabel Mercer could run the gamut from "Mandy" and "I'm a Little Blackbird Looking for a Bluebird" to "Feelin' Groovy."

Mabel might never have made it to America without the help of Marion Barbara Carstairs, known everywhere in the international set as Jo. It was the charitable Jo who financed Mabel's trip to New York.

Jo Carstairs was an heiress of extravagant wealth, owner of a succession of yachts and an island in the Caribbean, a gay woman who made no secret of her sexual proclivities and preference for men's clothes. And stories about the Carstairs flamboyance were legion. She had met Mabel in the south of France—in

Antibes or Juan-les-Pins, one of the resort villages considered most chic in the years before World War II. It was there that Jo had been a houseguest of Grace Moore, the American soprano.

One evening the two were invited, along with Marlene Dietrich, to a starchy formal gala

Mabel Mercer and me on the set in South Carolina where we made our TV special.

somewhere along the Riviera. Dietrich and Moore met for cocktails in the salon, wearing their most elegant Parisian gowns, and
waited for their friend. When she came down the stairs, the two
stars were aghast. Jo was done up in impeccable black tie—dinner
jacket and trousers, wing-collared shirt—the works. To be greeted
with "You can't go out with us in that getup—for God's sake, dig
up a dress!"

A short while later an unchastened Jo appeared on the stairs
once more, this time wearing an evening gown as stylish as those
of her two friends—and equally décolleté. Now the shock was even
more horrific. Jo Carstairs's arms were embellished with tattoos.

"Back, back!" shouted Grace Moore and Marlene. "Back to
your room and put on the tuxedo!"

There was an impressive list of glittering ladies who went to
Paris to find fame and fortune in the years before World War II—
starting, of course, with Josephine, the legendary "La Bakair."
Some of them never came back. Some did. And some, like Mabel,
happily adopted the United States as their native land.

I came upon Blanche Dunn back in the Mars Club days. She
had given up acting in 1933, after playing a small role in the film
version of *The Emperor Jones* with Paul Robeson. The beautiful
Fredi Washington told me why, describing the scene in which the
two women were supposed to stage a fight, and Blanche complained that Fredi's performance was far too forceful. This led to
the early retirement from the boards of "La Belle Blanche"—and
her decision to choose another life—in Europe, of course.

Soon after I met Blanche in Paris, she was whisked away by
her current "protector" to a luxurious Capri villa. His jealous wife
appeared, killed him, and committed suicide. A major scandal,
even for that scandalous island in the Mediterranean. Blanche
stayed on, making Capri her home ever after. I saw her there once,
near the end of her life. Despite a stroke, Blanche remained a great
beauty, though a fading one, dressed in pale, floating chiffon under

the protection of a delicately colored parasol. We walked. She asked about mutual friends in a fragile voice. "How is Mabel? How's Jimmy? Bobby, how do I look?" She stopped for a moment, turned to me, and then we went on. "How's Mabel—how is Jimmy? How do I look, Bobby?" And she kept glancing at herself in boutique windows along the way before repeating the same questions again and again. "How's Mabel—how do I look?" A fight in the movie made from a Eugene O'Neill play had been much too real for her, I thought, but a sense of personal theatrics had never deserted her.

It was Blanche who had introduced me to Elisabeth Welch, in Paris on a winter night in February. It was snug and cozy downstairs at Spivy's East Side, and Liz had come from London on her way to the south of France. She had the English notion that the Riviera was *unbearable* in summer, that it was far more suitable to escape there from the London winter; hence her stopover in Paris. I couldn't wait to meet the singer who had introduced "Solomon," Cole Porter's outrageous song in *Nymph Errant* in the early thirties. After hearing her recording, I had added the number to my act and had great success with it. I had also heard that Welch was very elegant and sophisticated. Suddenly there she was, next to Blanche on a banquette just across from the piano. All smiles and extraordinarily beautiful in her furs. She lived and worked in England and was eager to hear about old friends in her native New York. Mabel, Jimmy, and Cole Porter, people in Hollywood—while she talked about her thriving career in London.

One night at the Red Carpet Mabel appeared with her old friend Bricktop, another of the illustrious women who ran famous cabarets in Paris Hemingway days. Brick was short, vivacious—and redheaded. We were in tune instantly, and from then on she paid me a visit wherever I worked. She appeared during one of my engagements at the Blue Angel, and I asked why it

With Mabel and Bricktop at Dottie's late-night watering hole.

had taken her so long to come by, having heard she'd been in town for a while. In a soft and reverent voice she explained. "The death of the prince," she said. I was aware of her fondness for European titles, but *which* prince? I wondered. "Why, the prince of peace, Pope Pius the Twelfth!" A Catholic convert, Brick had reverently avoided nightlife for a respectable length of time after his death.

I used to see another one of these remarkable women when I was backstage at a revue called *Black Broadway* that I appeared in and co-produced. It was during the second act, and the great tap-dance group called the Copasetics were on stage, dancing to the twenties hit "I Can't Believe That You're in Love with Me." There, in the wings, I found one of the show's stars, Edith Wilson—survivor of a long and successful European career, who had been coaxed into returning to the stage. Edith was waiting to go on. She stood there singing along with the orchestra in a low voice, little more than a murmur. Her whispered rendition startled me, and I asked, "Edith, you're singing that song in German?"

"Of course, dear," she replied. "In the old days we always sang in the language of the country where we performed. French, Spanish, German—whatever."

As she spoke, she gave me a level-eyed look that clearly questioned my question. The kind of look my mother had given the Short brood when matters of decorum came up. Decorum— meaning propriety, correct behavior, the fitness of things. More than manners. To know who we were and to act accordingly. No head hanging. Back in high school, when I considered it a tremendous plum to be chosen to sing a leading role in our a cappella school show, I preened about playing a train conductor in a railway station scene. I was going to sing "When That Midnight Choo Choo Leaves for Alabam'." Oh, no, I wasn't, said my mother. Not Mrs. Short's boy Bobby, not while she was alive. And I had to tell the teacher I wasn't allowed to sing what my mother called Jim Crow lyrics.

I'll never forget her trying to hide her satisfaction as she heard the applause after one of my first amateur performances. She would not applaud—oh no, it was not proper to cheer for one of your own. I have an indelible memory of the look on her face when she read my report cards. I knew how proud she was of her Bobby— proud the first morning she led me into the kindergarten class, proud as she brushed my hair before sending me off to first grade.

She worked all her life, Myrtle Short did—with a dignity that was astonishing. From seven in the morning until the early hours of the evening—whenever the job was done. And she never missed PTA meetings, class day exercises, or church. No easy feat when she had only Thursday afternoons off.

She had no objections to jazz—after all, Uncle Bill, her brother, played fine ragtime—but she had no use for the blues. No, not that music filled with sexual innuendo. I had heard an instrumental of "Shake That Thing," but I didn't get to hear Ethel

Waters sing it until I was out of high school. Mother taught us the importance of probity and of pride and orderliness. The importance of a clean, starched shirt.

Yes, indeed, Mrs. Short had firm ideas about behavior. And to this day I hold on to her philosophy of what is just not done. Like public displays of emotion. Bad manners. Temperament. Which is why I have always treasured my privacy; it is something that belongs to me—like self-respect and self-esteem.

One evening at Sam LeTulle's house on Sutton Place, the piano was moved to the edge of his lawn, facing the East River, for a garden party. One of his guests surprised me with requests for song after song from my repertoire. A few weeks later at a party given by Iva Patcevitch and his wife, the same man requested a dozen more favorites, and we were introduced. His name was Peter Sharp, and he was an amateur pianist with a love for my kind of music—and he had just bought the Hotel Carlyle. I knew the Cafe Carlyle was a smart and quiet room where a great performer named George Feyer had been ensconced forever. Peter Sharp and Ahmet Ertegun were best friends. Not long after we met, Sharp showed up at the Living Room with Ahmet and his wife, Mica. And three days later my phone rang. Someone from the Carlyle asked if I might consider filling in for Feyer sometime in the spring. Don't get excited, I said to myself—too many offers had come my way in the past, only to fade into limbo.

Then Peter Sharp called, confirming a two-week engagement in April. And, of course, my sidemen—Beverly Peer on bass and Richard Sheridan at the drums—must appear with me.

I've been looking the landscape over
And it's covered with four-leaf clover.

Ira Gershwin never wrote truer words. Things were looking up, way up.

New York
1968—93

eorge Feyer went off on his holiday, and I replaced him for the two weeks. Then the Carlyle management came up with an offer for me to play there for six months of the year—alternating with Feyer. This prompted George to move to the Stanhope, a charming hotel opposite the Metropolitan Museum on Fifth Avenue. And so my romance with the Carlyle began—little did I dream it would last for twenty-five years.

Eubie Blake once said that a performer is *on* from the moment his audience sees him. That thought crosses my mind every night, as soon as my cab passes Seventy-second Street, before I ask the driver to pull up behind the limos on Madison Avenue and Seventy-sixth so I can slip into the lobby from the side street without running into a crush of people. I go up to the third-floor room to check my clothes, put drops in my nose, and get downstairs again. But if there is a group in the lobby, I meet them and greet them—gratefully. Eubie was right. After all, these people are my audience—the folks who applaud me, who pay their money to come into the cafe. The years have taught me they are all my friends.

Madison Avenue was considered "uptown" when I began at the Cafe Carlyle. A smart hotel, more than smart—the Carlyle epitomized New York in its best conservative style. Architecturally, the clean line of the building warranted talk of making it a landmark. The elegant simplicity that was all the rage in the late twenties was evident in the interiors: the influence, no doubt, of two prominent designers of the time—Syrie Maugham and Elsie De Wolfe. Everything about the hotel had an aura of old money.

The first year at the Cafe Carlyle was unforgettable—and successful. The manager was Harold Bock, whom I had met back

Preceding page: In my flat at the Osborne with two prized possessions—my Bechstein and painter Ronaldo de Juan's smashing acrylic.

at the Sheraton East. Mr. Bock was old school, as traditional as the Park Avenue hotel that had once been the Ambassador. He came by every evening to check out the details, running his hands across the potted plants to look for dust, examining the place settings ready for the first dinner patrons. I heard him explain the new style of entertainment to somewhat irate old customers. Speaking in French, he told them that, though the kind of music now being presented in the cafe was not quite what they were accustomed to, times had changed—and all the while he was fingering the philodendrons.

"A cover charge? Outrageous! Don't you know my parents were married in this hotel?" Once I heard this said, but times did change. The cover charge remained, and the clientele adjusted. The customers, old and new, kept coming in.

The aura of the Carlyle endured as New York grew and neighborhoods changed. The city spread out, stretching south to a new area called SoHo, then farther downtown to a district called TriBeCa. After a time New York became more than my home, it was *my* town—and how I loved it. I bought a bicycle in 1969, and the Peugeot became my limousine. I'd ride as far north as Hamilton Terrace up in Harlem, travel down to the Battery, and sail across the harbor on the Staten Island ferry. I'd ride through Central Park and take trips to the Village, where my buddy, Tad Adoue, lived in an apartment off Fifth Avenue. I even pedaled to work—although it was hell on my dinner jacket.

Madison Avenue at Seventy-sixth became an extension of midtown when shops like St. Laurent, Givenchy, and Versace opened. There were new restaurants along the side streets and new art galleries, after Parke-Bernet was launched just across the avenue from the Carlyle. Boutiques, haute couture, and antique shops arrived, pushing farther and farther uptown, past Eighty-

On my Peugeot on the way to Central Park.

Top row, left to right: John Barry Ryan, Lewis Lapham, Bobby Short, Bill Styron, Bruce Jay Friedman. Second row, left to right: Nicholas Pileggi, Robert Brown, Jean-Pierre Ransam, Buzz Farber. Third row, left to right: Willie Morris, Jack Richardson, Elaine Kaufman, Chris Cerf, David Halberstam. Fourth row, left to right: Arthur Kopit, Jack Gelber, George Plimpton, Gay Talese.

sixth Street to what is now called Carnegie Hill. It was a busy, jumping neighborhood that took on new pizzazz when Elaine Kaufman moved from the restaurant she'd worked at downtown in the Village and opened her own establishment on Second Avenue, just north of Eighty-seventh Street. Elaine was a twinkly-eyed lady round enough to be called Rubenesque. With her fast-take humor, fabulous skin, shining intelligence, New York street smarts, and earth mother warmth, Elaine was an arresting personality. She was aided and abetted by Elaine Stritch, who, briefly, came in to help her namesake and was surely the most glamorous bartender in town.

The first customers were journalists, novelists, and a group of show business people, most of them aspiring or just on the verge of making it. Her customers became her friends—no one will ever know how many meals she bought or the drinks she offered on the house. Soon Elaine had her crowd, not unlike the faithful crew that came to see me week after week, month after month—and now, year after year. In the beginning there was many a night when business was not overwhelming. The place might be empty too early in the evening, and Elaine would close the door and say we should take off for P. J. Clarke's, where there was sure to be more action. But word of mouth spreads quickly in the city, and soon the place was packed. Before you knew it, Elaine was a hostess running a salon on Second Avenue—and, as the saying goes, anyone who was anyone was going uptown to Elaine's.

When Irving Penn photographed her for *Vogue* wearing sables, and surrounded by the men in her life, all of us looked pleased as punch to be there with her.

Beverly Peer, my bass player for years, said something once that I've never forgotten: "I'm here for the reason, not for the season." And I remember those words when my throat acts up or, worse, when disaster strikes during a performance. I've learned not to take the night's high jinks home with me. The rowdy customer is not going to remember in the morning, I tell myself, so why should I?

Phil Moore used to maintain that a careless bartender could ruin a magical moment, that a clumsy waiter approaching a customer might kill a punch line. Here on my perch I can see every corner of the room, and after all these years Ambrose and I have developed a special language. I can signal with nothing more than a slight gesture, a flash to tell him that something is wrong—with the lights or the sound—with a nervous patron near the tiny stage.

I'm always aware of who is leaving, who is coming in. I learned this watching Mae Barnes at the Bon Soir; she was always conscious of the flow, constantly on the lookout. A hangover from those days when a dollar was hard to come by in a club, when the weekly paycheck was not always guaranteed. I'm still reminded of Danville, when I was a kid falling asleep on the piano, until the headlights flashed as a car pulled up to the roadhouse, alerting me to get on with another popular song of the moment. That was quite enough to give me a sixth sense about performing, to know that—borrowing from Gertrude Stein—a saloon is a saloon is a saloon.

Saloons—that was how Abel Green, editor of *Variety*, the show business bible, categorized all cabaret and supper clubs. I couldn't agree with him more. For years I have been calling the places I work in "saloons." Even the Carlyle is a saloon. A place that sells liquor. Not just one of the dives you see in a Hollywood western, where the hero has the shootout with the villain as the dance hall girls go on with the show and the brassy leading lady with a heart of gold sings over the sound of flying bullets.

Nor does it matter how fancy the decor is, how elegant the service, how excellent the cuisine, or how exclusive the clientele— the place is still a saloon, with the most difficult task presented to the performer, and maybe the greatest reward. Where else is the response so quick, so overwhelming, that it might knock a performer off his feet? Despite a smoking, drinking, talking mob—if you are lucky enough to have drawn that big a crowd, nothing is quite as satisfying as gaining the attention of a nightclub throng.

Time is short in a saloon, and within minutes I have to establish a rapport with the audience. And, having won that rapport, I must not allow them to lose interest.

Professional saloon singing takes talent, experience, and discipline. Discipline for me begins as soon as I am up in the morning. The day is made up of preparation for going to work, even to having my main meal at lunchtime and not another bite after that. Sometimes, though, I am tempted. I often think of what Betty Comden said when we talked about performers' regimens. She told me that Rex Harrison's formula was to have a small tin of fresh Beluga before a performance. Energy giving, low calorie—and totally glamorous.

In the beginning at the Carlyle, thoughts of caviar were far from my mind. Becoming a movie star or a television personage were dreams I had back in the forties—I suppose everyone in show business has had those fantasies. Then the fifties brought reveries of Broadway stardom. But I came to realize that saloon singing was my métier and the Carlyle my natural habitat. That synergy eventually would make the Carlyle the quintessential international saloon; no other city can boast of such an establishment. When anyone said the Carlyle, the name *Bobby Short* came to mind automatically.

This modest cover charge shocked old patrons in the beginning. It has escalated steadily over the years.

Back in 1958 I had rented a triplex studio on the eighth floor of Carnegie Hall, just around the corner from Phil Moore and just across the roof from a new friend, Peter Duchin. There I could play the piano all night long if I wanted to. I had no furniture when I moved in, only half of a Ping-Pong table Phil lent me, a used Steinway grand he had found for me, and a new mattress. Later David Long would come by to build shelves for the records and books that were taking over my space. David was one of those

Carrying my antique pier mirror from Carnegie Hall over to the Osborne.

jacks-of-all-trades who often came to my rescue. Fourteen years later I moved across Fifty-seventh Street to the Osborne, the landmark co-op built at the end of the last century. I found an apartment that had belonged to André Watts—I could still play the piano all night long. Later on a larger place became available: Leonard Bernstein's apartment when he was conducting the New York Philharmonic at Carnegie Hall, in the days before Lincoln Center.

By that time I had more furniture—thanks to a few of my friends. Tad Adoue gave me a Chesterfield sofa, Howard Perry Rothberg lent me a pair of handsome chairs. And I now owned a Ronaldo de Juan; my Argentinian pal was an accomplished artist, and he presented me with a smashing outsized acrylic painting.

I was in business. A new Bechstein grand was ordered, its delivery delayed until I sold my used Steinway and was settled in the new apartment. However, one piece of furniture was quite a problem, an eleven-foot-high pier glass that I wouldn't trust to a commercial mover and that I couldn't move without the help of a couple of friends. Off the wall it came, into the elevator, then down eight floors and into the street. Ronaldo and Bobby Nahas, the restaurateur, gave a hand lugging the piece across

Fifty-seventh Street to the Osborne, where we had to repeat the operation in reverse. A street cameraman found the sight of us worthy of a photo—a shot of a huge mirror moving across the crowded sidewalk with only three pair of feet visible.

When I began my life in Carnegie Hall, two good friends, Sonny and Michael Rosenberg, thought I should have a cat. The

On the roof at Carnegie Hall with Rufus and Miss Brown.

atelier, with its balcony and a roof just outside the upstairs, seemed perfect for feline habitation, and after much urging, I agreed to visit a fully grown Abyssinian male at a downtown pet shop. There I discovered mutual love at first sight—I brought the cat home that same afternoon. Rufus Rastus Johnson Brown, Rufus for short. He took over immediately, running up and down the stairs at a wild pace, tightrope walking along the narrow balustrade on the balcony, obeying commands like a dog. In no time at all he became my constant companion, even going along with me on short trips. A few years later the Rosenbergs had another suggestion—Rufus needed a friend, and they had seen a female Burmese kitten in the same shop. "Why not call her Miss Brown?" they asked, and I took their suggestion. Miss Brown was an ornament to the household, though she never warmed to me the way Rufus had. But then she didn't have much chance.

When I moved across to the Osborne, the "Socialites" came with me. I had taken to calling them that, since nothing pleased them more than the admiration of guests as they preened and pranced around. I saw the pair through minor illnesses, taking care to leave them watched over when I was out of town. One fall I came back from Europe to find Rufus in bad shape. Visits to the vet were in vain—he was, after all, seventeen years old and visibly feeble. Shortly and inevitably, he died. I really loved Rufus, to the point of refusing for months to acknowledge that he was gone. A few years later Miss Brown died. I always felt that she was lonely without her beautiful and spoiled mate. And it was a long while before I could bear the thought of owning another pet.

Years later, when I was about to move across town to Sutton Place, I decided to take on a poodle. A royal, the biggest of the breed. A reputable kennel in New England promised me a male puppy from the next litter, and the new arrival came by air to LaGuardia. There I encountered a frightened ball of black fur, delighted to be out of his cage and on my lap. Buster became his name, and he took to his new surroundings instantly, growing into a handsome specimen who attracted attention wherever he went. Twice a year Buster accompanied me to France, where even the French were awed by his beauty and good sense. One summer, following the advice of a new veterinarian, I flew to France without giving him his customary sedation. He seemed a bit dazed when we arrived, and I was surprised that, after the long flight, he was not at all interested in water. Soon he wouldn't eat. After two weeks of animal hospitals and clinics, his kidneys failed—and I watched him fade away. Afterward, with French pomp and circumstance, my housekeeper, Madame Clement, removed his bowls and his toys. It was a sad summer chez Short.

I came back to New York that fall, sure that there would be no more pets for a while—until Mary Lee Settle invited me to Virginia for a weekend. The celebrated author of *The Beulah Trilogy* lives in Charlottesville with her husband, Widdy Tazewell, and a pair of handsome Dalmations, who greeted me with thunderous barking and wild tail wagging. I told the Tazewells that Buster was gone, and it didn't take long for Mary Lee to say, "You should have a Dalmation, Bobby. You look like a Dalmation person."

Enter Chili. Not long after our weekend, Widdy was at my door, carrying a small box with a lively black-and-white bundle inside. He had driven all the way from Virginia to spare the puppy any anxious moments. I named Chili for a pretty actress of the forties called Chili Williams, whose press agent had insisted she'd be a sensation if she wore only polka-dot dresses, which she did during her very brief career. To this day Chili does not know for whom he was named, and I don't think he'd mind. At seven, he has a personality all his own. He is well-known around Sutton Place, and most often he is spoken to by other dog owners before his piano-playing walker is greeted.

More and more I realize how much I like what I do. The evening is always brightened when I hear "Hello, Bobby, this is my wife—this is my daughter." And quite often I am surprised by the arrival of some old friend I haven't seen in years. These days

New Yorkers seem to make up about half of our nightly Carlyle crowd; the rest come from other parts of the country—even the world. I see a familiar face. I hear, "Bobby, may I introduce you to my mother . . ." or, "Meet my son. . . ." Someone from out west or down south, Canada, Mexico. People who are all dressed up and smiling and remembering some other time, wanting to pass on their warm, fond memories to a younger someone at their side.

"Mr. Short, you seem to be having such a good time up there." Mr. Short. I like hearing that, too, particularly from a young person. "You can't possibly call it work!" I feel that work is a privilege, carrying on a tradition. One handed down from Duke and Count Basie, from Lena and Pearl Bailey. Which reminds me of a night, when Pearl walked in with Louis Bellson as I was winding up a set. For my last number I sang "Don't Like Goodbyes," a song she had introduced in *House of Flowers*. I then took my final bow and went over to their table. After a kiss for my compliment, the lady offered the ultimate Pearl of wisdom when it comes to an audience and a performer: "But remember, Bobby, always leave them with something that they know."

One day at lunch Betty Lee Hunt asked me who came to the clubs I worked in, what group followed me from saloon to saloon, who were my strongest boosters. We were just beginning the permanent press relationship that has lasted up to today, and I told Betty Lee there were three groups—show folks, what was once called "high society," and the fashion crowd. Ever since the Haig, I have had a following from the creative worlds that are the ornaments of civilization, and I've always thought that fashion and theater had a lot in common. What other lines of work depend so heavily on fantasy and make-believe? Nothing is more entertaining than a well-produced, high-style fashion show. It can take on all the glamour of a Ziegfeld revue.

I met Geraldine Stutz during my first year in New York,

With the stylish Geraldine Stutz at El Morocco.

before she reshaped the image of Henri Bendel, the elegant specialty shop on West Fifty-seventh Street where she made retail history with bravura worthy of a theatrical impresario. A charismatic, take-charge lady with great personal style, Gerry became one of my great friends. I soon learned to appreciate her caring intelligence, her respect for talent, and her insatiable curiosity. And we have never stopped sharing our love of everything that makes New York fabulous.

Eve Orton, another fashion friend, had been married to John Weitz, the noted designer. An editor at *Harper's Bazaar* who was born in Vienna, she came here during the war and had a keen eye for style. Eve used to drag her friends into all the saloons I worked, and she became a regular at the Carlyle. Eve made fashion predictions, and they always came true—where the hemline was going, whether women would wear pants. Some of her edicts were unforgettable—heavy is not warm, she said in her soft, lilting accent. Eve was unforgettable, too. Besides John Weitz, my fashion buddies included Bill Blass, for whom I often modeled in the sixties; Ralph Lauren, who long ago handed me a perfect navy blazer that, patched and worn, I still treasure; Donald Brooks, whose greatcoat in fur I wore for a *Harper's Bazaar* sketch; and Helen O'Hagan, Saks Fifth Avenue's longtime public relations whiz. When Jean Muir's elegantly understated clothes came to New York from London, it was a great day for Muir fans. I'll never forget the first time I saw a collection of hers at Bendel's. When I think of that afternoon, I remember an old Porter tune— "Is It the Girl or Is It the Gown?" The gowns that day were splendid, but so were the girls. One stood out particularly—her name was Renee Hunter. The color of a new penny, and just as bright, she's been a shining addition to my life ever since. When she tired of the runway, her fashion expertise led her to her own business, representing young designers.

With the elegant Eve Orton on my birthday.

love performing, but I've always found it exciting to be on the other side of the stage, to be out front watching the performance of a talent that I—out of conviction and admiration had sponsored.

I discovered that when I presented Jane White at Town Hall. For a long time I had been impressed watching Jane on stage. Her sense of comedy was superb, her timing was terrific—and, when I saw her do a cabaret act, I thought she was a singing Cornelia Otis Skinner. No higher praise: Skinner was one of the great monologists of all time. And Jane was no disappointment; her concert was a success. And the notices were equally good for the Amherst Saxophone Quartet when I presented them at Carnegie Recital Hall, where they played everything from Bach to Eubie Blake transcriptions.

Then George Wein suggested an evening with Jean Sablon at Lincoln Center, and I joined him as producer. The man who was called the French Bing Crosby had been a favorite of mine when I was in my teens and had he worked with the renowned Stephane Grappelli. Sablon's reception was enthusiastic, and I had no idea that in a few years he would be my neighbor in the south of France.

In 1980 I was again part of a team with George, producing *Black Broadway*, a revue celebrating performers who had lit up the Great White Way in the first fifty years of the century. The incredible cast of evergreen talents included Edith Wilson, John W. Bubbles, Honi Coles, and Eubie Blake, along with Elisabeth Welch and Adelaide Hall, who came from England to join the company.

In 1927 the very pretty Adelaide had been on a bill with Duke Ellington and his band. She and her husband were standing in the wings at one performance, listening to Duke's "Creole Love Call." The trumpet solo was played with a mute, innovative at the time, and Adelaide began to sing a countermelody. Duke came into the wings to say that was exactly what he'd been looking for. And when "Creole Love Call" was played in the next show, Adelaide

With Julie Wilson, Harry Roy, and the legendary Leslie "Hutch" Hutchinson during one of my London sojourns.

sang it, this time on stage. In a later recording session, Adelaide's voice became part of a duet with the clarinet in an improvised scat—and musical history was made. In 1929 a leading role in *Blackbirds* brought Adelaide to Paris, then to England, where she was embarked on a truly remarkably career.

I never think of London without remembering Leslie Hutchinson. I had heard about him since I was twelve years old. A black crooner from the island of Grenada, he had become a household name in England with his own radio show, hundreds of records, and a unique cabaret career. His elegant manners and wardrobe made him a favorite with the English upper crust and the British royals. In the thirties he entertained at the Lido in Venice for Cole Porter's parties. It was years later that I met him with Julie Wilson, when I was at the Astor Club in London, and at last I had the opportunity to see him work at Quaglino's, a smart boîte off Jermyn Street. He had a great feeling for jazz and he was matchless with the popular hits of the day.

It was an extraordinary cast assembled for *Black Broadway*—young Gregory Hines shared the emcee duties with me, and Nell Carter rounded out the company. Mercedes Ellington, Duke's niece, staged the dances, Dick Hyman and Frank Owens handled the orchestrations. The show was wonderful, the precursor of the black-entertainer wave that crested in *Ain't Misbehavin'* and *Black and Blue*. But contractual problems caused us

The all-star cast of Black Broadway on our sad closing night.

Dancing at the Carlyle with Alberta Hunter.

to close in four weeks. Then, once more with George Wein, I produced the last of Jimmy Daniels's records. It was a fine album, a fitting swan song for that most distinguished man-about-town and enchanting friend.

I had heard of Alberta Hunter, but we hadn't met until I gave a bon voyage party for Mabel Mercer to celebrate her first trip back to England since the thirties. Mabel asked me to invite Alberta, and when George Wein's assistant, Charley Bourgeoise, realized what splendid form she was in, he called Barney Josephson, who booked her into the Cookery, his Greenwich Village restaurant club. Alberta, who hadn't sung for years, was a sensation. I booked Carnegie Hall for her concert debut, prepared ads, and arranged for Gerald Cook, the brilliant accompanist, to work with her. It was all set—but Alberta's last illness forced us to cancel.

My summertimes have long been spent lying in the supposed lap of luxury in the south of France, where, with a little imagination and enough red wine, any dream is possible. But after the garden has peaked and those first few hints of fall are in the air with great reluctance I have to face who I am and think about what makes me tick. I think about going home to the tightrope existence, to getting up and going to sleep on schedule, eating properly, and doing two shows a night, where I look forward to those nightly gab sessions with Barbara Carroll over tea before our first sets begin.

To celebrate my first four years at the Carlyle, Peter Sharp, with Ahmet and Mica Ertegun, gave a party. Taking their theme from my Cole Porter album, which had just been released, Mica and Chessy Rayner decorated the Trianon Suite with blowups of Horst and Hoyningen-Huene photographs—Garbo, Josephine Baker, Vernon Duke, and Cole himself. The guests were asked to come in thirties dress, two orchestras played, champagne flowed. Roy and Aminda Wilkins, Maxime de la Falaise, Eve Orton, Ruth Ellington, they all came. So did Elaine Kaufman and the Andy Warhol crowd, along with Truman Capote. Had my time at the Carlyle been up that night, I could have walked away feeling on top of the world.

Nightlife at the Carlyle rolled on. I can still see Gary Merrill dropping in, wearing walking shorts, sneakers, and a sweatshirt. The maître d' refused to let him have a table, and the following night Gary came by again, this time in black tie. With no problems, he was given a table, where he promptly ate the steak sandwich he had brought with him.

Alice Faye and I greeted each other like old friends, no introductions necessary, and she came in often during her stay in New York. One night I made sure she was seated close to the piano, then fastened my lapel mike to her blouse, and in her husky voice she sang "You'll Never Know"—to a fantastic reception from the crowd.

I'll never forget Ambrose handing me a note from Jacqueline Onassis with a request for me to play "I've Got Five Dollars." As I was going through the song, I saw her having a giggle with Ari Onassis.

Jessye Norman, Shirley Verrett, Beverly Sills, Leontyne Price—these divas have all been in to see me. And, incidentally, I was at the piano, full of pride, accompanying Eileen Farrell at Beverly Sills's farewell gala.

A long way from a morning at Nellie and Harold Brown's house in California. Television was a great novelty in those days, and it gave Nellie a new way to serve her meals. A tray for each of us in the living room in front of the set. We were having breakfast on a late Sunday morning—Nellie's delicious pancakes—and we weren't paying much attention to what was on the screen, but we were grabbed by the Puccini music. We were looking at the *NBC Opera Workshop*, a production of *Tosca*—and Leontyne Price was singing the role. A first! This was before Marian Anderson broke the color line at the Metropolitan, and we were a teary and thrilled trio, sitting there in the Browns' living room.

The charisma of a star is hard to describe—a magical, ephemeral something that goes along with the knowledge gained by experience. And for a singer, one prerequisite is perfect diction. You understand this when you listen to Mabel, Ethel Waters, or Bessie Smith. I can still hear Avon Long's exquisite diction as Sportin' Life in *Porgy and Bess*.

A pianist and singer named Larry Carr had an uncanny knowledge of popular American music, and he knew all about the great singers of the past. He produced records, putting together a number of albums evoking a bygone era—and he was a great stickler for diction, for respecting a lyric. He talked about singers he'd known who would join words together sloppily, giving them an altogether unintended meaning. Like Jerome Kern's "All in Fun," with the line "Some orchids, some cocktails, a show or two . . ." Larry knew a performer who had slurred the words and come up with "Some more kids, some cocktails . . ." And another who read Sondheim's lyric as "Send in the clouds . . ."

Then there's Marian Anderson's dear, definitive story about the minister at the Baptist church who had become aware of the unusual generosity of one of the sisters in his congregation. Sunday after Sunday she dug into her purse to put an impressive amount of cash in the collection plate. Wanting to thank her in a special way, he approached her after services one morning to ask if the choir couldn't sing a special hymn in recognition of her outstanding generosity. The sister reflected for a few seconds and meekly replied that her favorite hymn was "Andy." The minister shook his head and allowed as he'd never heard of the song, but that he'd consult with the head of the choir. The choirmistress, too, shook her head, and with this sad news he returned to the sister, who insisted she had heard the piece sung many times before. He asked if she would hum a few notes to give him an idea of how it went. She complied readily with her own interpretation of the venerable Protestant hymn: "Andy walks with me, Andy talks with me, Andy tells me I am his own."

I jumped at the chance to appear with the Barnum & Bailey Circus at Madison Square Garden one year. Riding under the big top on an elephant's back was irresistible—but there were union problems, and I was asked to be a clown instead. With a carrot-colored wig and a bulbous nose, I was part of the never-ending crowd that poured out of a tiny old car—and then I was one of the policeman-clowns, with a billy club that I could use with wild abandon because it was made of cloth.

Circus music or Sondheim music—I always hear music. It is the subtext of my life. Radios and records and tapes sound out all day long when I am at home. I work out with music and eat with music, and in that rare hour or two when I have the sound equipment turned off, a tune is always playing in my head.

I communicate through the words I sing and the tunes I play on the piano. People often think that the songs I choose reflect my own mood of the moment—that what I'm singing may have to do with my own angst or happiness. Or that I sometimes sing a particular song to someone in the audience.

Guest clowning with Ringling Brothers Barnum and Bailey. I'm the one with the spiffy four-in-hand foulard.

Perhaps *for* someone, but never *to* anybody. My personal emotions are private. Working in a saloon or concert hall is not my idea of privacy. When I am thought to mean every word I sing, I consider it a compliment, meaning I have given a true acting performance.

Not long ago I was talking with Claudette Colbert, who has proven notions of her own about the craft called acting. I had just been sent a script for a dramatic role in a television series, and I was expressing some trepidation about accepting an acting job.

"What in heaven's name do you think you've been doing all these years, Bobby?" she exclaimed. "Just approach the script the way you do your songs, and you'll be perfectly fine."

I was to appear as a fading cabaret performer in a segment of Carroll O'Connor's television series *In the Heat of the Night*. The character was called Ches Collins, and one of his songs contained the clue to a murder he'd witnessed years before. With Claudette's coaching in mind, I gave it my best shot. And it must have worked—the same character was brought back for another episode, in which Carroll O'Connor cast me opposite the incomparable Jean Simmons in a tender, nostalgic romance.

What pleasure Claudette's friendship has brought me, her warmth never more front-and-center than the night she was honored by the Lincoln Center Film Society. That evening a stellar group came to pay tribute to her glorious film career—Irene Selznick, Claire Trevor, Kitty Carlisle Hart, Gregory Peck, Ray Milland—and I hoped I was giving her a happy surprise by bringing Fredi Washington as my date. The two had not met since they'd made *Imitation of Life* in 1934, and it was a loving reunion, touching to see them greet each other with such joy.

When Woody Allen was making *Hannah and Her Sisters*, he asked me to sing "I'm in Love Again," Cole Porter's song, for a scene at the Carlyle. A few years later he asked permission to use my recording of "I Happen to Like New York" over the titles of

Claudette Colbert and Fredi Washington at Lincoln Center in their first reunion since Imitation of Life.

Manhattan Murder Mystery. I played myself in a nightclub sequence in the Michael J. Fox movie *For Love or Money*, and I went to London to play a jazz musician with Michael Caine in *Blue Ice*, a part with a running relationship like that of Rick and Sam in *Casablanca*. Me and my piano! Imagine, after all these years—playing dramatic roles, I am in the movies.

But I wonder if there is anything that makes a face as instantly recognizable to the public as a television commercial.

The advertising agency handling the launch of Revlon's perfume Charley called one day to discuss my doing one. When I arrived at the agency office, my recordings were piled high on a desk, a jingle was played for my approval—and in no time flat we were doing a recording. The next week the video portion was filmed at Hippopotamus, one of the trendy East Side discos. I sang the new song, and I met Shelley Hack, the good-looking model hired to sashay into the club as I played. We were an overnight success—the commercial went on to run for nearly ten years—my face was flashed all over the country, then all over the world. Nothing I'd done before made me so recognizable—from then on wherever I performed, club or concert hall, I was "that guy in the Charley commercial."

Not like the one movie I had done back in the fifties. *Call Me Mister* was based on a Broadway revue starring Betty Garrett. Before the film, every available black performer in Hollywood was screen tested for the "Going Home Train" number, featuring one of Harold Rome's hit songs. I got the part, and the rest is—a very obscure bit of Hollywood trivia.

I once played a game of movie trivia with Shelley Hack in Washington. We were going back to our hotel in a limousine after an evening at the White House, and we were naming Ronald Reagan movies we had seen. I thought I was winning because I remembered *Love Is on the Air*, a forgettable film from the thirties, but Shelley topped me, with all the Reagan westerns she had watched on television. That was the night I told her that this time it hadn't seemed like I was singing for my supper in the White House. I had had a call from Nancy Reagan, her voice warm and cheery. She was planning a dinner party for Charles, the Prince of Wales, in a few weeks. Nothing grand, she said, just four tables of eight in the private apartment of the White House. Would I come for dinner with a date and perform for thirty minutes afterwards? I would, I did, and Shelley and I had a memorable evening.

The first time I heard from Washington, my nephew Ted was working there, his involvement in national politics a matter of immense pride to the Short family. One afternoon he was on the phone, asking if I'd be interested in performing at a presidential party. He was promoting a group of teenage singers from Watts called the Young Saints, and would I sing on the same program with them? At a dinner for the Duke and Duchess of Windsor. At the White House! I said yes, of course—and the action began. The phone rang like crazy—the White House, the Washington press, the columnists—question after question about my politics and what I was going to sing.

Vic Damone, Liza Minnelli, and I croon it up in the East Room at the White House, while Marvin Hamlisch pounds the piano.

I am used to out-of-town gigs, and this, I told myself, was going to be merely one more night playing at a private party. But panic set in on the fateful day. Who was I kidding? This was my first time at the White House—and I wanted friendly faces around me. I asked Betty Lee Hunt's assistant, Henry Luhrman, to come along with me and my two musicians. My old friend and boss at the Gala, Jimmy Hulse, was in New York, and I invited him. My brother Reg and his wife, Earleen, were coming, too. After all, they were Ted's parents, and this was a major event for the Short family.

Rehearsals went smoothly enough, but the kids from California—all thirty of them—looked as if they hadn't had a decent meal in days. We had been asked to sing, but the White House was not offering us supper.

Today I cannot remember how cool or how nervous we were as we stood waiting downstairs while the guests were at dinner. Surely the "backstage staff" with their complex security measures were daunting while we waited outside the East Room. At last the Nixons and their guests emerged after coffee in the Red Room, and the duchess spotted me in the hall. "Oh, David, there's Mr. Short," she cried out, breaking loose from the group. Suddenly I was being greeted by the Duke of Windsor and the Nixons. An unexpected way to meet the president of our country.

The Young Saints disappeared into the East Room, which had been set up with gold ballroom chairs facing a stage. The soul singing of the group created an almost churchlike atmosphere that brought down the house. Mr. Nixon introduced me with ease and charm, mentioning that I was from Danville, Illinois—and the performance went quite well. We posed for photographs, but I found myself thinking of nothing but food. The kids from Watts were not the only hungry ones. The White House staff went into action, and a reservation was made at a restaurant not too far away. Cars and a special bus got us to a late supper. All thirty Young Saints with their organist and music director, my group of

Bobby Short
With deep appreciation and best wishes,
Patricia Nixon   Richard Nixon

Wallis
Duchess of Windsor
Edward
Duke of Windsor

My first appearance at the White House when President and
Mrs. Nixon entertained the Duke and Duchess of Windsor.

family and friends. Luckily, I had tucked a credit card into the
inside pocket of my tailcoat.

Six years later Washington summoned once more, now it was
President Carter's office on the phone. Would I come to the United
Nations for a dinner to honor a group of European foreign minis-
ters? It was an interesting request: the president wanted to hear
songs by Gershwin. Then, a few months later, another call came
in from the White House—this time a bid to come to Washington.

The Carters' style of entertaining was quite different from
that of the Nixons. Most obvious to me was the absence of black
ties. Clearly, Jimmy Carter's attitude was more relaxed and casual

Waiting my turn to shake President Carter's hand; behind me is my sister, Mildred Stratton, looking starry-eyed and just a little incredulous.

than that of any administration before him. On a hot afternoon he was in his shirtsleeves, leading me off on a personal tour of the White House, food was being barbecued on the lawn, and he called me "Bobby"—a familiarity I didn't dare return. My date for dinner that night—yes, the Carters had asked me to dinner—was my good friend Gloria Vanderbilt. She was as thrilled about being there as I was.

Not too long after, another invitation came, this time to be a guest, with no request to perform at all, at dinner for Prime Minister Ohira of Japan. And I thought it was time my sister Mildred had a taste of Washington high life. How pretty she is in the photograph that was taken that night, standing just a bit behind the Carters and me. Looking slightly incredulous, but I'm sure it was an evening she remembered for the rest of her life. I had shown her the splendid art deco grand piano in the front entry—an impressive instrument with American eagle legs—and it made me proud to sit down and hammer out a tune on it.

The Carters made me feel as though I belonged there, and I was sad when their term in the White House ended.

Now, on a clear night in May, Shelley Hack and I had turned into the drive leading to the northwest gate of the White House. We were greeted by the Marine Guard and led into the Grand Foyer banked with red, white, and blue flowers. Up the splendid

My third visit to the White House—this time with the Reagans.

Grand Staircase to the private chambers of the First Family, the rooms where our presidents and their wives have lived since the nineteenth century.

We reached the top of the stairs, a string quartet was playing show tunes, and we made our way to the yellow Oval Room. President Reagan stood at the door, greeting each punctual guest with a firm handshake and a gesture toward where Mrs. Reagan waited with the guest of honor, His Royal Highness, the Prince of Wales.

Dinner was superb, coffee and liqueurs were served in the hall, and the president ushered us back into the Oval Room, transformed into a miniature concert hall. I had asked Mrs. Reagan earlier to give me a sign when she felt I had been on long enough. No signal came—the Reagans stood at my final bow, all smiles and warm thanks. Prince Charles came forward to say that he found the Porter, Coward, and Fats Waller I'd sung much more appealing than many current songs. After that observation he could do no wrong as far as I was concerned. Champagne continued, along with bubbly conversation. Mr. Reagan told us about the forgotten antiques discovered in the White House storerooms, and talked to us about his early days in Hollywood. No wonder Shelley and I agreed we had been to a magical party.

Musical trivia and tracing show tunes became a hobby of mine long ago. A useful pastime, considering how many people revel in the out-of-the-way, obscure, and just plain forgotten or discarded Broadway show tunes. Many of my friends love to play the game of singing a few lines and asking the group to guess what show the song is from—the same game I first played with Jean and Dorothy, Bob and Dick, in Paris. It isn't at all uncommon for someone to send me a piece of music in the mail from a show that never saw the light of day after an out-of-town opening or, worse, never made it to the stage in the first place. To this day I attempt to be faithful to the composer's line—true to the lyricist as well. Time is short in a saloon, so I make no complicated references, and I never natter on about the original production.

I can still hear "God Bless America" announcing evening curfew at the Radio Room in Los Angeles, the first night Don McCray walked in. He always kept in touch, from the time he had worked for a talent agency when I was a kid. And, though he was in the U.S. Army Special Services Division, he found time to become more than a coach—I suppose he become my mentor. Don gave me advice about projecting a lyric. He arrived at the Browns' with piles of sheet music I was not able to read. He found great songs from musicals that had flopped and was the first to say how good a number would be for me to perform. He used to take the trolley out to the house, carrying stacks of new records to play on the Browns' phonograph. It was Don who introduced me to the inimitable sounds of Mabel Mercer and Cy Walter. Don McCray taught me musical taste, opened my ears to more music than I can possible list. I play numbers today he found for me then and through the years.

One Christmas I received two record albums from Wayne Collins, a steady customer wherever I was playing back then—an album of Lee Wiley singing Rodgers & Hart songs that most people did not do, another of Greta Keller performing out-of-the-way material to Cy Walter's accompaniment. Wiley combined an innate jazz sense with impeccable lyric taste. Keller mixed obscure French and German songs with her American choices.

Greta Keller had been singing in smart clubs since the mid-thirties, charming her audiences with a cabaret style evocative of that other time when small clubs thrived in Berlin and Vienna. It was said she had a hand in creating Marlene Dietrich's singing style. And her glamorous presence more than made up for her small voice. Greta claimed to be Viennese, though rumor had it she was denying her German origins because it did not suit the political climate of the time. In the thirties there were many rooms for acts like Greta's, but the competition was fierce, with much jealousy, rivalry, and bickering. Word was she'd stop at nothing to oust other performers. Years later, as I sat with Mabel Mercer one night at a club, listening to Greta sing, I couldn't resist asking her, in French, what Greta's nationality was. Mabel whispered back, in French, "Viennoise," and then, after the slightest pause, added, "je crois."

As a kid, I remember promising myself to learn three things: to drive a car, to swim, and to read music. After years in California, the first was a necessity. And eventually, a swimming coach called me "pool safe." As for the third, I long ago bowed to Erroll Garner's sagacity—for himself as well as for me. "Man," he said, "who in hell's gonna hear you read!"

Pianists who sing have always been around; so have singers who play the piano. Performing may be the most mobile of all entertainments. If there is a keyboard to pound, the pianist will find it—be it spinet or upright, baby or concert grand. Even as a kid back in Danville, I always found someone in the crowd able to beat out the latest tune and more than a few ready to contribute a lyric. I am still amazed to discover how many actors can play a piano. Think of Kevin Kline and Michael Moriarty, and Diana Lynn, who had quite a way with the eighty-eights. Holly Hunter did not need a double to play for her in *The Piano*.

Maurice Rocco used to dance while he was at the piano. Rex Evans, a huge man who sang "Harlem on My Mind" for Garbo, and Hope Emerson, no petite person herself, accentuated their avoirdupois by working with tiny portables that they pushed around the nightclub floor. I've never used my elbow to stress a point, the way Dorothy Donegan does, nor have I rocked the piano back and forth and then stripped for my finale the way Johnny Paine did before his exit at the Blue Angel.

I still sometimes get a wild case of nerves before I sit down at the piano. Sometimes the anxiety attack comes when I'm to perform in a new atmosphere. It happened when I was asked to appear with the Boston Pops, under the direction of Arthur Fiedler. For three Cole Porter concerts, my first time with a symphony orchestra—talk about exciting! This glamorous gig came about because of the Porter Album I'd made with the Erteguns— just two musicians with me, no fancy artwork, and a mighty impressive reaction from the public—helped, of course, by Robert Kimball's album notes. The album led to television programs, a New York concert—and the Boston invitation.

At the first rehearsal Arthur Fiedler looked at the opening song on my list and glared at me. He wanted to know when the orchestra was to begin, to see the first four bars on manuscript paper. I obliged. After that and everything seemed to go smoothly, until the contralto, Karen Armstrong, complained of a sore throat. She muddled through our first evening but was too sick to go on the following night. Dr. Fiedler met me at the door in a panic— what was he to do? Since the contralto range is not too far from my tenor, I went into a huddle with baritone Richard Fredericks, who was the other guest. And the concert came off with a tenor and a baritone, gazing into each other's eyes in front of the full symphony orchestra and crooning, "Till you let me spend my life making love to you, day and night, night and day!" The good-sport audience gave us an ovation.

It wasn't until months later that I looked at the conductor's sheet for my music that had thrown Arthur Fiedler for a loop. There on the page were the first four notes of "Why Shouldn't I."

Earlier, the pinch of orchestrations, a conductor, and a stage

Some of my favorite ladies (clockwise, from far left top):
Elaine Kaufman, Sisi Cahan, Jean Bach, Jessye Norman,
Claire Trevor, and Lynn Wyatt.

manager cut into my modest salary and ended making no sense at all. In the seventies I had offers from a California friend to do concerts in Los Angeles and San Francisco. My old friend Tom Hatten, the actor and singer, lined up theaters and I made trips out west to the Wilshire Ebell Theatre, then to the Shubert and the Dorothy Chandler Pavilion, and to the Geary and Curran in San Francisco with my two backup musicians. Then Richard Swig of the Fairmont Hotel chain entered the picture. He persuaded me to try a few weeks at the Venetian Room of the Fairmont in San Francisco. Thrilled to have a chance to work in a large cabaret, I asked Dick Hazard to come up with new orchestrations. And for the next few years I went off to the Dallas and Atlanta Fairmont hotels. My old pal Russell Orton, a canny production pro, came along as stage manager—until the Fairmont cabarets closed. Finally I filed away my orchestrations, calling it just one more adventure in my peripatetic career.

George Wein thought it would be smashing for me to appear with Duke Ellington at Carnegie Hall, singing songs made famous by Ivie Anderson. Mercer Ellington and I discussed the numbers—"I Got It Bad," "It Don't Mean a Thing"—we went over the orchestrations and the keys, though it all seemed rather casual to me. The musicians were late because of a traffic hangup, and before we finished rehearsing, the audience was streaming into the hall. But I had the time of my life, singing the songs of my idol. And to see Duke standing with both hands resting near the bow of the concert grand as I performed was a moment I shall never forget. At the start of the rehearsal, Harry Carney, Duke's star saxophonist, had asked me what I was planning to do. He smiled when I told him it was to be a small tribute to Ivie. "She'd be mighty proud," he said, and I was truly touched to hear him say that.

In the company of music greats and mentors—Eubie Blake, Cab Calloway, and Lionel Hampton.

Thinking of Ivie and Duke Ellington makes me see Billy Strayhorn, though he has been gone for many years. He was the perfect complement to Duke. I was in Danville High when I first came across his name. Billy was the genius who melded his own musical ideas with those of his acknowledged hero, Mr. Ellington. Billy was called "Sweet Pea," and with Duke he produced a sound that made the entire jazz world sit up and take notice—just think of "A Train." His work for Ivie Anderson was nothing short of stunning, and he made his mark with "Lush Life," "Chelsea Bridge," and "Don't Get Around Much Anymore." When I first heard his tremendous innovations in Danville, I'd often put my own lyrics to some of his instrumentals. I've always considered it a privilege to have known the shy little man from Pittsburgh with the sparkling eyes behind enormous round glasses. I can hear the soft, almost purring low voice, bright with subtle humor—Sweet Pea was supremely hip. Like a Sulka tie. You had to understand the quality of the silk, the aesthetic of the pattern. If you didn't get it, you didn't wear one. And you missed something unique. Like Sweet Pea.

Carol McCallson was a very special person, one of the first models to arrive from California in the fifties, along with Catherine Cassidy, Patty Enk, and Anne St. Marie. The pages of *Vogue* and *Harper's Bazaar* were brightened by photographs of her taken by Derujinsky, Scavullo, and Helburn. A glamorous job, but Carol always reminded me of the grueling hours and near slave status a fashion model endured, at the mercy of the editor, the stylist, the client, and the photographer. We first met when she commuted from Glendale to Los Angeles. Discovered by Richard Engstead out there, she came into the Haig with photographer Bill Claxton. Always seated immediately in front of the piano, they practically shared the pink gel glow of the spotlight with me. Carol's Scandinavian features were chiseled, suggesting Garbo with a hint of Carole Lombard. Slouching (as they did in those days), wearing her peasant blouse, her broomstick pleated skirt and sandals, with a Phelps leather satchel over one shoulder, she asked if I knew the Rodgers & Hart "How Can You Forget?" To know those first lines—"How can you forget when you lie awake and dream at night, how can you forget when your heart has a mosquito bite . . ." told me how hip she was. She knew New York

This was a photo I'd asked Horst to do as a Christmas gift to Carol.

back then, all the right names, the right songs. She was opinionated as all hell, and fiercely loyal. Later I discovered her insecurities, but her vulnerability only made her more appealing. She and Bill stayed until closing time, and then they drove me home. She said she dreamed of my coming to the big city. And from the moment I arrived she was my champion, coaxing everyone she knew to come see me.

Carol made sure every photographer had a copy of my first Atlantic record; it was played at every photo session. Bill Helburn said he'd warned her that if she played it once more, he'd destroy it—she did, and he kept his word. Not only did she bring an appreciative crowd to see me, but I was assured of having the best-looking audience in Manhattan.

Carol married Bertrand Taylor III. A match made in heaven, everyone said. Bert came from a stylish, slightly raffish old New York family. In the twenties, his father had squired Gertrude Lawrence when she came to New York, and acquired star sartorial status as the first man to wear suede shoes on the floor of the stock exchange. Bert's aunt Dorothy, who married the Italian Count di Frasso, later was linked with Gary Cooper and Bugsy Siegel, two fellows who could not have been more opposite. Carol and Bert seemed such good casting that everyone was sorry to see the marriage come to an end. But there was Daisy—the delight—their adorable daughter.

One day Daisy asked me to perform for her class of fourteen-year-olds at the Chapin School. Each student was to present a favorite experience from her recent vacation, and I was Daisy's choice. I agreed, and proof of the success of my half-hour stint came the following weekend, when a suspiciously young group of couples sank onto the banquettes at the Carlyle, no questions asked, as their shining adolescent faces faded into the darkness when I began my show.

My bookings were diverse—from an afternoon at a school on Manhattan's East Side to a flight to Columbus, Ohio, for a fund-raiser at a venerable department store. F&R Lazarus was redecorating part of a floor to look like the Carlyle, even to the ashtrays ordered from the hotel. All this to benefit the local arts council. Not since the forties had I played in a store, and then it had been a completely different gig. I played piano at the May Company in Los Angeles, as models strolled a runway, because a friend knew how much I needed the cash.

Evelyn del Barrio was the May Company fashion director who had glided into a club one night while I was working, her platinum-gray hair piled high into a topknot, wearing a Dior dress and a captivating smile. Evelyn adored high life, spoke brilliant Spanish, and loved to dance the rumba. We'd sweep in and out of the clubs out there on the Strip, places I'd never been to before, and she saw to it that I met everyone she knew. Then, when I was out of work—not an uncommon condition in those days—she hired me. Clever Evelyn even put me behind a folding screen for a lingerie show, so I could see the models and cue my music, but the decorous audience never saw me. She is now Evelyn Lambert, living in Europe, and I see her most summers. Though not nearly often enough.

Top: Jimmy Hulse peering around my "sold out" concert poster.
Above: Backstage at L'Espace Cardin in Paris with Ronaldo
de Juan, Rafael Lopez-Cambil, and Paloma Picasso.

Lovely Lena Horne and glamorous Alexis Smith give me a kiss at the party celebrating my twenty-fifth year at the Carlyle.

One morning I looked at the calendar and realized that it had been twenty-five years since Jean Bach and I first met at the Sherman Hotel in Chicago. A celebration was in order, and we decided to give a supper dance at the Carlyle. All too soon fifteen years skipped by, and we hired Count Basie and his orchestra for another blast at the hotel to commemorate a fortieth anniversary. Our guest list kept growing, and we needed the grand ballroom at the Plaza for a fiftieth-year party. A Sunday afternoon tea dance with Jean in chiffon, two orchestras to supply the music, and everybody dancing. I wonder what we'll do when the big six-oh comes up.

I first saw Mougins in the seventies, discovering it on vacation in the south of France when we had a meal at the Moulin de Mougins, one of the roster of three-star restaurants in the area.

A lazy village with the locals out early every morning preparing for the lunchtime onslaught of tourists, a village out of a movie operetta. It was love at first sight. There was a mill for rent off the main square, decorated by someone from Dior in Paris, with a patio facing the twinkling lights of Grasse off in the distance when night fell at nine-thirty. After a summer there, I wanted a place of my own. Advice from Jean and Bob Bach helped, George Huycke came down from London to offer counsel, and in 1983 I found exactly what I was looking for, outside the old town. A modern house, all stone and glass with tiled floors. A bathroom for each of the bedrooms, a big garage, and a wine cellar. A footpath led to the village. I still had a view of Grasse—and the price was right. Besides, it had been named Villa Manhattan.

Voilà—I was a landowner, with a house on the Riviera. Sisi, Mary Sykes Cahan, was with me the day I signed the papers; we

Fredi Washington, Jimmy Daniels, Jean Bach, and Alberta at the Bach/Short fortieth anniversary party.

were barely able to stifle our laughter as we listened to the interpreter saying I was *borned* for the villa since Manhattan was my home.

The day after tomorrow I'll be there. The garden will be blooming, and I'll be hearing the afternoon silence broken by the shouts of children from the nearby school. The loveliest way to be disturbed. A house full of friends for the summer. Nothing can be better. Down from London come Liz Welch and Jean Muir and her husband Harry Leuckert. Fred Astaire's daughter Ava arrives from Ireland with her husband Richard McKenzie. Geraldine Stutz and Bobby Nahas, Marti Stevens and Sisi Cahan pop in from New York bringing all the latest news from Gotham, and Andy Athy comes over from Washington, D.C. along with Daisy Taylor and young Will Helburn. Occasionally, Charley Cochran exchanges the Palm Beach sun for a few weeks at Villa Manhattan. And there are the pals who live nearby. The Stevensons, Isabel and John. The sculptor Armand Arman and his wife, Corice. Robert Courtright

George Huycke and Jean Muir—perennial visitors at Villa Manhattan.

who paints and Bruno Romeda who sculpts. Selma Ertegun, Marian Shaw, Alex Cohen and Hildy, the Broadway producers, and Dalton Baldwin who has accompanied every major singer on the concert scene. Sometimes Hank vanAmeringen ventures out of the sweltering Paris summer to peruse the brocantes and restaurants nearby. And in the old days I was never surprised to see George Huycke arriving in his mini-wagon accompanied by his favorite blonde, Mae, a willful labrador named for you-know-who. Sometimes they showed up with two more good old friends in tow, Fred and Ann Lyon of San Francisco. Nor will I forget the endless luncheons with Jimmy Baldwin and Bernard Hassell who always arrived by taxi from St. Paul de Vence since neither gentleman drove. Tom Parr and Klaus Scheinert in that knockout house and garden in nearby Opio. Estelle and Carl Reiner, Kappy and Bill Leonard, Sue and Lester Wunderman, photographers June and Helmut Newton, Joyce and George Wein and Dorothy Gerard and Carol and Joe Lebworth. We are near family there in the warm Mediterranean air. I look forward to the invitations that may come from Mary and Harding Lawrence or the Marquise Mia de Riencourt or the Countess Donina Cicogna and Tiqui Atencio to visit them in their sumptuous showplace residences. And of course my great pals from Texas, Lynn and Oscar Wyatt. The beautiful Lynn swept me under her protective wing where, with Oscar's approval, I've remained ever since. No summer on the Riviera would be complete without a string of dazzling parties with these kind and generous friends.

And I'll be seeing Cimiez Park in Nice, no trip complete without a visit to the Roman amphitheater, the Matisse Museum, and George Weins' ten-day festival called the Parade du Jazz when all the greats of the jazz world gather to play. There, near the monastery, surrounded by olive trees, is the very special monument that I found nearly twenty years ago, a bronze bust of Louis "Satchmo" Armstrong. Coming upon it that first time was thrilling—and thought-provoking. In the States we had given no such honor to a jazz musician.

A few miles away in Antibes, I discovered the likeness of the great clarinetist Sidney Bechet. I made up my mind to see that like homage would be paid to my idol Duke Ellington. That fall my attorney friend, Raoul Fielder, and I formed the Duke Ellington Memorial Fund. Its purpose was to found a fitting memorial to the Duke in New York. Another old friend, Patty Enk—now Patricia Faure, who runs a gallery in Southern California—was quick to point out that only one artist should do a larger-than-life Ellington bronze. Sculptor Robert Graham was the obvious, sole, perfect choice.

Now, six years and three mayors later, after an endless approval process, countless bouts with park commissioners and community boards, and a dozen fund-raising drives, Graham's sculpture will be installed on the Duke's birthday in the fall of 1995, at the corner of 110th Street and Fifth Avenue. A most fitting site, I think, since the Duke's world embraced both his beloved Harlem and the world beyond.

As a kid in Danville I used to stroll down Vermilion Street, gaping at the store windows and ducking into a movie house whenever I had a spare dime. Today Vermilion Street is sparsely populated. Many of the old merchants have moved on to the local mall, others have simply given up, but one movie palace remains. A few years ago a group of local citizens formed an organization to raise money to save the lavish old Fischer Theatre. As a fund-raiser, they asked a few of the hometown fellows who'd made it in show business to appear together. There I was with Donald O'Connor, the Van Dyke brothers, Dick and Jerry, and Gene Hackman; we put on our dog and pony show, and quite a lot of restoration money was raised. That evening we were invited to the old Hegeler mansion on Vermilion Street. I hadn't been inside the house since the thirties, when I performed after dinner at the fam-

With Dick Van Dyke, Donald O'Connor, Jerry Van Dyke, and Gene Hackman at the landmark Hegeler mansion in Danville.

ily's fancy parties. Their children—Madelle, Eddie, and Julius— used to sit on the first landing of the staircase, listening to the music and laughter long past their bedtime. Long past mine, too— I was only a child myself.

Part of me is still that child, still the little kid in knee pants going up to the balcony of the Fischer Theatre in Danville, waiting for the first movie show of the day to begin. The houselights are still on in the ornate gilt-and-velvet interior, and the rickety sound system is playing that old recording of "There's Danger in Your Eyes, Cherie." In a few moments the song will be over, the lights will go all the way down, and I'll be in make-believe land, hanging on to every word, every image, and certainly every song until the final fade-out, until I see those words spread across the screen—*The End.* Then I'll get up to stretch, buy a box of Cracker Jack, and go back in to wait for it to happen all over again.

Photograph Credits

The authors wish to thank the following for the use of their photographs. If not listed below, the photographs are from Bobby Short's personal collection.

PAGES ii, 3, 14, 28, 37, 51, 69, 90, 123, 147, 178, 201: Francesco Scavullo PAGE 6: Bruno of Hollywood PAGES 18, 52: Maurice Seymour PAGE 30: *Life* magazine PAGE 92: Wally Seawell, Paul Hesse Studios PAGES 126, 138, 148, 164: William James Claxton PAGE 141: Reprinted by Permission of *Ebony* magazine, copyright 1964 by Johnson Publishing Company PAGES 190, 214: Freidman-Abeles, Willard Avery Photos PAGE 211: Dottie Frank PAGE 218: Eugene Cook PAGE 220: Irving Penn PAGE 233: Lewis PAGE 239: Gerry Yulsman PAGES 241: Paul Schumach, Metropolitan Photography Services, Inc. PAGES 252-253: *Women's Wear Daily*, Fairchild Publication, Press Photos, Starr Black, *New York Times* PAGE 257: Horst PAGE 259: Pepe Fernandez PAGE 262: Harry Leuckert PAGE 265: Rich Stefaniak, *Danville Commercial News*

Permissions